The Changing
Image of Woman
in the Novels of
Shashi Deshpande

The Changing Image of Woman in the Novels of Shashi Deshpande

H. RANJITA

Prestige

an international publishing house

Published by
Prestige Books
New Delhi 110 058
Ph. 011-25507139
email: prestigebooks@gmail.com
website: asiabookclub.com

Associate Office
60/29-45 Parramatta Road,
Concord, NSW 2137
Australia

ISBN: 81-7851-088-X

Printed at Chaman Offset Press, New Delhi 110 002

Contents

Acknowledgements

Perhaps the most striking feature of contemporary fiction is the emergence of feminist literature. This branch of literature is feminist not only in the sense that it is written by women novelists but also because it gives expression to the sufferings, aspirations and hopes of women in a world dominated by men. The novels of individual writers like Arundhati Roy, Anita Desai and Shashi Deshpande are realistic in the sense that they are relevant to real life as opposed to romantic or escapist writing.

Shashi Deshpande, one of the foremost Indian English novelists, is the winner of the prestigious Sahitya Akademi Award for her novel *That Long Silence*. Her novels portray the middle-class Indian woman who is undergoing a gradual transformation in terms of her position in society. She presents a realistic image of woman in her writings. Her novels resonate with real life experiences, are refreshing and reflect the social fabric of India's life. Her emphasis on the importance of being self-independent reflects the kind of feminism she projects through her women protagonists. The relevance of her feminist concerns to the present-day Indian society triggered me to write this study.

The present volume offers the possibility of drawing certain common patterns in the growth and development of women characters who make conscious efforts that ultimately lead them to attain their selfhood and identity, marking a new beginning in their lives. The book evaluates the entire corpus of Deshpande's fiction, including the recently-published novels *Moving On* and *In the Country of Deceit*. It makes a rich contribution to the corpus of Women's Studies, Sociology and Indian English Fiction.

I cannot close these prefatory remarks without acknowledging my gratitude to all those who have helped me in the preparation of the present project. I am grateful to Professor M. Mani Meitei, Department of English, Manipur University, Imphal, for his generous guidance, valuable suggestions and the kind of academic training imparted to me. I owe my sincere thanks to Professor S. Sanatombi Singha, Department of Manipuri, Manipur University, for her encouragement and valuable advice. I am grateful to my loving parents-in-law—Shri R.K. Manisana Singh and Smt. R.K. Apabi Devi, Thangmeiband Polem Leikai—for their encouragement and moral support which are, in fact, invaluable to me. I owe my heartfelt gratitude to my loving and revered parents—Shri H. Ibobi Singh, retd. Principal, Hill College, Tadubi and Smt. H. Shanti Devi of Khundrakpam Makha Leikai—for their encouragement and inspiration. My gratitude is due to all my well-wishers, friends, brothers and sisters, especially my eldest sister, H. Ranita Devi, Manipuri Department, N.B. College, Khundrakpam, for their co-operation. I extend my heartfelt thanks and gratitude to my loving and understanding husband, Major R.K. Shyam Singh, Indian Army, who despite his heavy commitments stood by me and extended all the help I needed. I thank Dr. Suman Bala of the University of Delhi who meticulously went through the book and to the staff of Prestige Books for producing the book elegantly and expeditiously.

Heigrujam Ranjita Devi

Introduction

As an Indian novelist writing in English, Shashi Deshpande's reputation has been on the rise. She was born in Dharwad, in Karnataka. Being a daughter of the renowned Kannada writer and Sanskrit scholar, Shriranga, she was exposed to literary world from a very young age. She graduated in economics in Mumbai and then gained a degree in law in Bangalore. She also took a course in journalism and for sometime, she worked on a magazine. Later, she took her postgraduate degree in English too. She started her writing career much later. She had dedicated most of her time to bringing up of her children. Writing seems to happen to her accidentally as she told in an interview:

> My husband was a Commonwealth scholar and we went to England. We were there for a year. I thought it would be a pity if I forget all our experiences there. So I started writing them down and gave them to my father. He gave them to 'Deccan Herald,' which published them promptly. So it began very accidentally. [1]

Her first publication that launched her career as a writer was a collection of short stories, *The Legacy* in 1978. Several volumes of the same genre follow it. She is also the author of four children books namely, *A Summer Adventure, The Only Witness, The Hidden Treasure* and *The Narayanpur Incident.* Shashi Deshpande has, so far, published nine novels. *The Dark Holds No Terrors* (1980), *If I Die Today* (1982), *Come Up and Be Dead* (1983), *Roots and Shadows* (1983), *That Long Silence* (1988), *The Binding Vine* (1993), *A Matter of Time* (1996), *Small Remedies* (2000), *Moving On* (2004) and *In the Country of Deceit.*

Acknowledging her talent as a writer, she was awarded the Sahitya Akademi Award for her novel, *That Long Silence* in the year 1991. Another two of her novels—*The Dark Holds No Terrors* and *Roots and Shadows*—have also received major awards.

Her writings are read and appreciated both at home and abroad. For instance, *The Legacy* has been prescribed for the graduate students in Columbia University. *The Dark Holds No Terrors* has been translated into a number of Indian and foreign languages. Though she began her writing career late, she has proved herself to be a competent writer, drawing her characters from the culture and society, which she had known very intimately.

As a novelist, Shashi Deshpande's forte lies in her realistic presentation of the life of women in general and the educated, modern, middle-class women in particular. She successfully makes an attempt to explore the inner 'psyche' of these modern women who are at the crossroads between tradition and modernity. She realistically presents the dilemma of these educated women who are struggling between the age-old traditional values, inflicted on them right from their childhood and the modern outlook they recently acquired from their education. Their condition seems to be worse than their past counterparts and those of present who still believe in these customs and traditions to which they submit themselves without any hesitation. Their problem lies in their inability to discard these traditional values at once and follow their newly acquired values. Most of her novels reflect predicaments and struggles of this breed of women.

As a creative writer, Shashi Deshpande does not create characters that are larger than life. She never creates strong women characters, as she believes in presenting them as they are. Her women protagonists are neither revolutionary in nature nor hysterical like most of the heroines of Anita Desai. In fact, they are ordinary women caught in certain situations that make them view and review their past life. By doing so, they realize, perhaps, the most important truth of their life that they suffer because they let themselves to be so. They had been blaming the society, the patriarchal culture for their lot, except themselves. All these years, they internalised the patriarchal norms and so conditioned themselves. They had been so blinded to see that "in this life itself there are many crossroads, so many choices."[2] Finally, they are able to hold the reins of their life. They know who they are, what they want and most importantly, how to get them. At the end, the protagonists are heading for a new beginning which is far better and more secure than before as they are no longer fearsome and dependent.

The protagonists are well aware of the exploitation of women at various levels and the prevailing double standard social, moral, cultural and religious codes that work against women as a group. They strongly condemn the oppressive system of patriarchy that binds them, curbing their rights as individuals. In this culture of male supremacy, craving for male child still continues. Even today, baby girls are not welcome and in some parts of the country female infanticide is still a common practice. From time immemorial, women have been denied the basic rights, sometimes, even the right to exist. It is no wonder that parents view their own daughters as "the visible symbols of their failure"[3] in a culture that firmly believes that whatever wrong is done by a man, his son frees him from it all. In *The Dark Holds No Terrors*, the protagonist, Sarita (or Saru), was exposed to such unequal treatment of boys and girls at very early age. She felt neglected when her mother showered all her love and attention upon her younger brother, Dhruva. She was taught that being a girl, she had to accept a second place even in her home.

The novelist challenges the prevailing double standard code of conduct of the society that has different scales for men and women. For instance, when a married man keeps a mistress or has more than one wife, society accepts it as a normal thing, but the same society condemns the same thing if a woman does it. In *Small Remedies*, Leela, a widow, is looked down upon by society and even discarded by her own family, calling her, "The black sheep of the family. A widow who remarried."[4] In the same novel, Ghulam Saab who had lived with another woman for years was warmly welcome, with open arms by her abandoned wife and family. Even the religious books maintain different yardsticks to govern the behaviour of men and women. The ancient scriptures like the *Manu Smriti* laid the foundation of such inequalities.

As a literary figure, Shashi Deshpande tries to deconstruct various myths and folklores constructed by patriarchy as an effective means to suppress women. Men, to consolidate their supremacy, created them and internalized these concepts in the minds of the women. The novelist provides a new perspective of these centuries-old myths. Unlike the images created by myths, she presents her women characters as human beings, not like the mythical characters, Savitri, Draupadi and Sita. All these years, women have been placed sometimes, on a pedestal and praised like goddesses but in practice, their condition is no better than that of slaves. Here, Deshpande seems to reflect what Virginia Woolf has observed:

> Imaginatively she is of the highest importance; practically she is completely insignificant. She pervades poetry from cover to cover; she is all but absent from history. She dominates the lives of kings and conquerors in fiction; in fact she was the slave of any boy whose parents forced a ring upon her finger. Some of the most inspired words, some of the most profound thoughts in literature fall from her lips; in real life she could hardly read, could scarcely spell, and was the property of her husband.[5]

Deshpande also deals with delicate issues like rape within and outside marriage. She exposes society's insensitive treatment to rape victims by looking them down as if they are the wrong-doers. Most of the time, the culprits get scot-free. Ironically, it's the victim's fate that is sealed as something derogatory but not that of the rapist. Such a case is realistically presented in the novel, *The Binding Vine* where the victim's mother, Shakutai tries to cover up the rape case as just an accident to avoid scandal that would ruin the marriage prospects not only of Kalpana, the victim but also of her other daughter. It is because society gives much importance to 'virginity' and 'intact hymen,' which is, of course, meant only for women whereas men have been given ample freedom in this respect too. Such unequal and partial treatment of women is being exposed in her novels.

As a novelist, it is quite a revolutionary thinking that she neither idealizes social institutions like marriage nor glorifies much-celebrated wifehood and motherhood, in a culture that gives much importance to these social positions. Unlike the militant feminist, Germaine Greer, who says, "If women are to affect a significant amelioration in their condition it seems obvious that they must refuse to marry,"[6] Shashi Deshpande feels the need to live within relationships. What she told Viswanatha is worth quoting: "It is necessary for women to live within relationships. But if the roles are rigidly laid that as a wife or mother you do this no further, then one becomes unhappy. This is what I've tried to convey in my writing. What I don't agree with is the idealization of motherhood—the false and sentimental notes that accompany it."[7]

Another aspect that the novelist successfully makes an attempt to express is women sexuality. Her women protagonists are conscious of their own sexuality. They regard it as a physical need and no longer consider it a taboo. Deshpande, through her protagonists, challenges the age-old notion that women have no passion and hence they do not have orgasm, a concept that has been/was supported by Western thinkers even. However, the very idea has been rejected by modern feminists. This is really gutsy on the part of the novelist to deal with such issue in a culture that denies women sexuality. Such discriminatory treatment of women is what the novelist is trying to focus on in her fiction. The women protagonists are also aware of the restrictions and impositions of the society over these matters on them. Women like Indu have to hide her sexuality and pretend to be passive as she realizes that it puts off her husband to find passion in a woman. Women have to suppress their sexuality and this adds to their frustration. Even in this area, gender discrimination operates.

The proposed book is an attempt to explore Deshpande's treatment of the women characters in her novels against the socio-cultural context of Indian society. Her writings reflect various genuine problems overlooked as ordinary little things. Deshpande seems to present these seemingly 'ordinary little things' as the basic tools fashioned and designed by patriarchy in the name of culture, religion and tradition to assure male supremacy and women subordination. Women have been trained right from their childhood to follow these man-made concepts and to perpetuate them among themselves. The novelist also exposes that it is not only men but also women who are responsible for the present lot of women and their position in the society as 'second sex.' In the novels, the novelist seems to reflect the struggles of women protagonists against such patriarchal systems.

Since this study concentrates on women characters and their experiences, two of her novels—*Come up and Be Dead* and *If I Die Today* are not studied as they belong to the detective genre which is quite different from the subject of study. Nevertheless, Deshpande's concerns about the inequalities and injustices meted out to women in our society are reflected even in this genre too and hence some references, here and there are also made. This study does not include the four children books she had written, as the subject matter and theme are of different kind. However, her short stories, because of their very nature and theme, are referred to here. In fact, the novel, *The Dark Holds No Terrors* is an extension of her short story, "The Liberated Women." The theme of rape within marriage is found in her story, "The Intrusion" and her novels *The Binding Vine*, as in the case of Mira, and *The Dark Holds No Terrors* in the case of Saru.

In her earlier novels like *The Dark Holds No Terrors, Roots and Shadows, That Long Silence, The Binding Vine* and *Small Remedies*, there is strong protest against the accepted standards and values, whereas, in her later novels—*A Matter of Time*, *Moving On* and *In the Country of Deceit* the novelist seems to deal such matters with great subtlety. In these three novels male protagonists are employed extensively and the novelist seems to preoccupy with human predicament, partially fulfilling her desire to write about human individuals not only about men and women only. Besides, themes like alienation, loneliness, frustration, are also dealt with in great detail. As a novelist, she crosses the boundary of personal or individual problems and tries to explore the human psyche and their loneliness, frustration, sentiments and emotions, the strength and weaknesses and most importantly their hopes and aspiration. Through these novels, Deshpande is able to come out from the closely limited private world of men and women to a broader universal world of humanity.

The book analyses Deshpande's concerns about the present position of women in general and educated women in particular. It also studies the novelist's attempt to expose the root cause of women's problems and subordination. Through her novels, she is consciously trying to put women on centre stage, pulling them out from the backstage where they had been pushed for many centuries. The book also studies how the novelist attempts to projcct the dilemma of modern women who have been struggling and enduring all forms of inequalities and injustices right from the day they were born in total silence much against their will.

It also discusses how various religions, culture, traditions and social institutions like marriage join hands to suppress women at various levels. Every novel seems to be the protagonist's quest for identity. It is in fact, a journey of self-discovery, self-realization and self-actualisation, a process of growth and development of the psyche of the protagonist from being dependent, fearsome and lack of confidence to her being independent, fearless and self-confident, a process of metamorphosis from being feminine to feminist. The main concern of the study is to analyse the novelist's attempt to project various responses and reactions of her women characters against the oppressive system of patriarchy and how finally they struggle to come out of the system to liberate themselves.

For the sake of convenience, the study and analysis of the novels of Shashi Deshpande in various light and shade will be divided into seven chapters. Chapter I is general introduction to the plan of the book and its core content. It is a nutshell of the whole study. Chapter II deals with a critical analysis of Shashi Deshpande as a novelist. This chapter attempts to study the various aspects of Deshpande as a novelist with special reference to her realistic, objective presentation of her characters, her views against generalization and politicalization of women's problems, her opposition to the categorization of women's writing where there are no such things like men's writing even if they happen to write of men's experiences. Deshpande here points out that discrimination of sexes opcratcs cvcn in the field of literature. Her style of writing, use of language, metaphors and constant reference to myths and folklores, connecting them to the present day from a new perspective, reveal clear departure from the long line of masculine tradition of writing. As a modern writer, she also deals with broader themes of human predicament, alienation, loneliness and lack of communication, emptiness and the theme of life and death elaborately.

Chapter III is an attempt to represent the social, cultural and literary milieu of feminism with special reference to its origin, movement, theory and criticism. It is an overview of Western feminist movement and its relevance and influence on Indian feminism as such. Chapter IV exclusively deals with Deshpande's treatment of women characters from the point of view of a feminist. Though Deshpande is a feminist as a person, she often denies being called a feminist writer as she feels it limits her writings and devalues other aspects of her novels. This chapter especially strives to study the feminist elements in her novels and also the kind of feminism she is trying to mirror in her work. As a feminist, she never takes the extreme stances that all men are bad and all women are victims. She sums up her idea of feminism in the words of Simone de Beauvoir "'the fact that we are human, is much more important than our being men and women.' I think that's my idea of feminism."[8] Though she admits to be an ardent admirer of Western feminists, she is practical enough to realize that it is difficult to apply Western feminism to Indian society as the socio-cultural and religious backgrounds, beliefs and sensibility are not the same. She does not appreciate militant feminism that discards social institutions like marriage, though she does not idealize or glorify them. She realizes the need to stay within relationship for the welfare of the individuals as well as the society. Her feminism arises out of society's unequal and partial treatment of men and women in all spheres of life. Hers is an objective feminism that acknowledges the strength and weakness, the goodness and faults of both men and women as individuals but Deshpande also realizes that there are certain areas where men exploit women and these areas are being highlighted in her novels. The fact that the treatment of women as a whole by the society is unfair and unjust is what the novelist tries to focus on. Her plea is to treat women as equals to men not as secondary or man's other. She points out how everyone—even parents, society, culture, social and religious institutions, film-makers, writers, painters, entertainers—consciously or unconsciously—contribute to the subjugation of women right from the time they were born till the last day. Hers is a feminism suited to Indian sensibility and favourable to Indian soil, yet it has universal appeal too.

The novelist depicts the struggle of her women protagonists from being dependent to independent persons. Her novels end with a new beginning for the protagonists to lead the kind of life they always wish to live. Society expects a woman to be an obedient daughter, loving and dutiful wife and caring mother only, and provides no room for personal growth and development. It is not only men but also women who need to fulfil their hopes and aspirations. Deshpande's feminism is a kind of following the middle path that works for a better relationship of men and women. This chapter attempts to study her treatment of women characters, especially the protagonists, from the perspective of feminism. The reactions and responses of these characters against the male dominant system of patriarchy are the main concerns of this chapter.

Chapter V, as the heading suggests, deals with the study of various problems and predicaments faced by educated Indian women in particular and women in general. The chapter is subdivided into four sub-headings. The first concerns itself with the common problems faced by women as a group. Women as a class are being treated as second-class citizens in every part of the world (though with some variations). Here the focus is on Indian women who have been suffering with silence from time immemorial. Female infanticides are still practised in some part of the country. Women have been taught and trained from a very young age to accept the secondary position even at home. The second throws light on the special problems faced by educated and working women. Working women are expected to do all household work starting from cooking, cleaning, washing to taking care of their children single-handedly. When they ever fail to do so, even their children blame them but not their fathers who do nothing at home. It's because even the children are so brainwashed by the society that household chores and child-care are the domains of women only. These modern women are suffering more because they are not able to follow these traditional roles whole-heartedly like their past counterparts and, at the same time, they are not able to discard them also. This is their dilemma and predicament.

The third sub-heading is about the specific problems faced by lower section of women who are not educated. Their suffering is doubled as they are colonized twice because of their own sex and, secondly, because of the class they belong to. The last sub-heading studies individual problems faced by individual women that cannot be generalized and studied as women problems. There are certain problems faced by certain women at a certain time that are purely personal and have nothing to do with problems faced by women in general. This is to avoid the danger of generalization of every problem faced by women.

The sixth chapter is an attempt to analyze the role and importance of economic emancipation to attain women's liberation. Here, both the positive and negative influences of financial independence in the power struggle within the family are taken into account with reference to the socio-cultural scenario of Indian society. In Western countries, economic independence is often considered as the answer and the solution to the question of women's liberation from the dependence syndrome. In our society too, economic independence works positively as a means towards women's emancipation in some cases but the deeply rooted culture and tradition of Indian society overshadows the light of economic independence. To cite an example, if the wife happens to earn more than the husband, both of them suffer as it is against the scale of the society. The chapter shows that financial independence of women is one of the important steps to women's emancipation but not the only one, considering the deeply rooted tradition and culture.

The last chapter is the conclusion of all the points discussed above with an emphasis on the general view of Shashi Deshpande's concerns about the conditions and position of women as reflected in her novels. Besides being a daughter, a wife and a mother, according to the novelist, women should try to prove their worth in other arenas. If half of the world's population remains in the shadow behind the remaining half, the world's progress would retard by half. Women should not confine themselves playing the allotted roles and following the dictated norms. They are equally qualified to try things at all levels. Men and women are not superior or inferior to one another but are different and should respect these differences in order to bring a harmonious and androgynous society. These are some of the ideas what the novelist seems to express in her writings.

NOTES

1. Viswanatha Vanamala, "A Woman's World . . . All the Way!" (Interview) R.S. Pathak, *The Fiction of Shashi Deshpande*, 233.
2. Shashi Deshpande, *That Long Silence* (Rpt. New Delhi: Penguin Books, 1989), 192.
3. Shashi Deshpande, *A Matter of Time* (New Delhi: Penguin, 1996), 151.
4. Shashi Deshpande, *Small Remedies* (New Delhi: Penguin Books, 2000), 45.
5. Virginia Woolf, *A Room of One's Own* (Rpt. New Delhi: Foundation Books, 2001), 51.
6. Germaine Greer, *The Female Eunuch* (Rpt. St. Alabama: Paladin, 1976), 319.
7. Vanamala Viswanatha, 236.
8. Geetha Gangadharan, "Denying the Otherness" (Interview), R.S. Pathak, ed., *The Fiction of Shashi Deshpande*, 254.

Shashi Deshpande, the Novelist

In this chapter, an attempt is made to situate Shashi Deshpande as a woman novelist who understands the plight of Indian women, and writes about them realistically and faithfully representing their authentic voice. Being herself a well-read person, she consciously writes from the point of view of woman about women's problems and predicaments, their hopes and aspirations, their feelings and sentiments. She is concerned with their silence, subdued anger and suppression under patriarchy. Her realistic presentation of women's lives and their problems and objective treatment of her characters—both male and female—earn her a niche among the contemporary Indian women writing in English. Her sensitive understanding of the suffering of women and its root cause, combined with her skill to present them authentically makes her a novelist with rare skill. She writes about women's problems, lives, their sexuality in an overt manner which echoes what Helene Cixous has once said regarding women writers: "Woman must write her self: must write about women and bring women to writing, from which they have been driven away as violently as from their bodies—for the same reasons, by the same law, with the same fatal goal. Woman must put herself into the text—as into the world and into history—by her own movement."[1]

In such a remark what appears pivotal is the underlying potential of women's body as a source of all generative power, the power to produce a female-oriented life and consciousness that would be able to recreate a female world with a female history in such a language that will subvert and upset the masochistic communicative language of man. As a distinctive woman writer, she is bent on a realistic presentation of her characters in that she seldom manipulates them, a quality that other distinguished writers do tend to stick to. She rarely portrays women as they should be; she rather seems to have a keen interest in portraying women as they are; as she tells Vanamala Viswanatha in an interview, "My characters take their own ways. I've heard people saying we should have strong women characters. But my writing has to do with women as they are."[2] Her commitment as a novelist is to give ample freedom to her characters who would lead their own lives with as little interference with their decisions and actions as possible. For instance, the sudden and untimely death of the protagonist, Sumi in *A Matter of Time* may not serve any purpose from the angle of women's cause and liberation or feminism which provoked such a comment from as eminent a critic as R.S. Pathak: "By removing Sumi prematurely from the fictional scene the novelist has denied herself the opportunity of bringing in the important issue of women's economic empowerment."[3]

It seems Deshpande's treatment of birth and mortality is never in conflict with the course of nature which means that she is quite content with presenting life as it is and reflecting "a slice of human life" in which, as she says "birth is there, death is there. Premature deaths we see all the time. Why people die we cannot say."[4]

Deshpande creates characters who live without their creator or following her likes and dislikes. They live in full freedom as individuals with minds and hearts as to determine what they are going to do with their self-justification. To cite one example, Sulu in *The Binding Vine* commits suicide because she cannot take the fact that it is her husband who has raped Kalpana, her sister's daughter. Deshpande justifies Sulu's suicide by saying, "Being the kind of person she is, for her, suicide seems to be the solution. . . . Human beings are made differently, we can't impose one solution."[5] Here the novelist seems to agree with Engels' realism as he says, "besides truth of details, the truthful representation of typical characters under typical circumstances."[6] Most of her characters live outside of her. They are living human beings on the pages of the book, not the patch board characters who would dance to the tune of the author.

In most of her novels, Deshpande tries to give a clear picture of genuine mother-daughter relationship too without any exaggeration and false representation whatsoever, at times, however, much against the popular notion built upon unreal dream and myth. More often than not, one finds the mother-daughter relationship depicted very lovingly and warmly in most of the fictions and popular media like films and T.V. Such representation, however, may not be constructed as real because in the first place, they are different individuals having their own preferences and tastes; hence the possibility of the clash of interest often catapulted into a generation gap between them, a fact that cannot be overlooked. All these intricate issues are kept engrossing in most of her novels. Her novels abound in good as well as not-so-good mother-daughter relationships. Vanna and her mother in *The Binding Vine*, Sumi and her mother Kalyani in *A Matter of Time*, Devi and her mother in *In the Country of Deceit*, share a good understanding between them; however the same is not the case with Vanna and her daughter, Shakutai and her daughter, Kalpana in *The Binding Vine,* Savitribai Indorekar and her daughter, Munni in *Small Remedies*, Jaya and her mother in *That Long Silence* and Saru and her mother (who have major conflict between them) in *The Dark Holds No Terrors,* Jiji and her mother in *Moving On*, Devi's mother and her grandmother, Rani and her daughter. The latter are an example where there is no smooth sailing between mother and daughter. What we find in such a treatment is that Deshpande as a novelist has an eye for different facets of such over-rated institutions and relationships of our society, and she cannot remain unconcerned. In this regard what she says in an interview is quite appropriate:

> I have a feeling that the [sic] people expect the love between mother and daughter to be very lovy and dovy. . . . It is a kind of image that we build up in Hindi movies. . . . Please look at the reality, I don't write from myths. I write from real life.[7]

In what Deshpande writes/says there is unalterable certitude that cultural myths, whether they are associated with man and woman, motherhood etc. are by no means similar to reality for they contrast and are opposed to each other. Myths are generally treated as cultural dreams, the idealized as against the real.

Shashi Deshpande's commitment as a writer seems to be away from that of a conformist, her politics is not hell bent like that of a hardcore feminist writer. She appears to be a bit shy of calling herself or being called a feminist or a postcolonial writer. Perhaps she feels threatened of being marginalized by such categorization from the mainstream literature. No doubt, from the various interviews she had given and the numerous essays she had written so far, it is quite clear that she is a feminist and proud to be one as a person. However, she strongly reacts against being labelled a feminist writer as she said:

> If I want to write about feminism and convey a message about it, I will not write a novel or a short story; I will write an article or an essay—as I have often done. But certainly, for women's writing to be judged purely as feminist writing is a problem.[8]

Yes, she writes as a woman about various problems being faced by women in Indian society, as a gendered class because of their sex, but that does not mean that she is a radical feminist accusing man of women's suffering and suppression, for man alone is not responsible for women's lot. The problems are of a multiple nature, and no single cause can be fixed as the root cause. The problems are dynamic and their treatment dynamic.

In this connection, it is not Shashi Deshpande alone who has taken this position. Eminent Indian women writers like Anita Desai, Kabita Sinha, Mahasweta Devi, Arundhati Roy, Nabaneeta Dev Sen express the same view, "there are good writers and bad writers, and gender is irrelevant in art."[9] They are of the view that such categorization separates them from the mainstream literature where a male writer "is hailed authoritatively and reverently, almost gloriously—as a writer. No hyphen, no prefix, no suffix. He is just a writer, prim and proper." [10] Even the Nigerian woman novelist, Buchi Emecheta writes, in spite of her very deep commitment to women's issues and problems that she would better be called a feminist with a 'small f.' Thus feminism is not aimed at separating women from men, it is a way of projecting women, women's image from a woman-centred perspective, and not a tug of war between the sexes.

Shashi Deshpande also reacts to a postcolonial situation in her being totally lost or deprived of identity, not a mode of expression against the dominant culture or Western/patriarchal construction based on the class, gender and race differentiation. We can see this as she speaks:

> Postcolonial too deprives me of my real and entire identity. It restricts the personal one to being the product of colonial rule and limits my writing to being no more than a response and reaction to colonialism.[11]

It is true that both feminism and postcolonialism are extreme political positions of resistance, subversion and counter-discursive practice. If looked at from this angle, Deshpande seems to shy away. Yet, her writing cannot be like that of Jane Austen, or George Eliot. She writes as an Indian feminist who does not fight for women's rights, privileges and equal treatment as was/is done in the West. Nor does she draw herself into that hub of postcolonial writing practice with the notions of centre and margin, self and other, master and slave. However, that situation can be applied to the man and woman relationship, women having been suppressed in similar colonial situation in the war of sexes. This aspect cannot escape our analysis many a time. Books like Mrinalini Sebastian's *The Novels of Shashi Deshpande in Postcolonial Arguments,*[12] argue that Deshpande may still be regarded as a postcolonial writer. Mrinalini Sebastian successfully attempts to study the novels of Shashi Deshpande by using the theory of contrapuntal reading of postcolonial theory. Reading and decoding of meaning depends upon, however, on the training and predilection of the critic who reads a text and deciphers meaning in the text.

Deshpande has reflected some of her attitudes and viewpoints on various issues and subjects through her protagonists. As M. Mani Meitei rightly states: "An artist is expected to design his work such as to represent life as he sees and understands it, partly or wholly true to his experience. No wonder then that certain characters speak like the author himself."[13]

Sometimes, it seems so obvious that we hear the voice of the author mingling with that of the protagonist. There are moments when the author is easily identifiable with the created character(s). It happens so because the writer is the creator of the character, hence there are always channels of thought commonly shared by the characters and the author. In speaking of her character's relationship with herself, Dorothy Richardson once made a statement that she was Miriam Henderson, in each of her words the author is there. Deshpande's demytholization of motherhood, as she speaks in an interview with Vanamala Viswanatha,[14] has been linked to what Urmila in *The Binding Vine* observes:

> Sometimes, I think . . . they brainwash us into this motherhood thing. They make it seem so mystical and emotional when the truth is that it's all just a myth. They've told us so often and for so long that once you're a mother you have these feelings that we think we do.[15] (76)

In another interview by Geetha Gangadharan, Deshpande says that intelligence is always a handicap for a woman. The same opinion can be heard from Indu's old uncle in *Roots and Shadows* that intelligence is always a burden. In her essay, "The Dilemma of the Woman Writer,"[16] Deshpande recalls how pleased she had been when one of her friends said that she had imagined the writer to be a man while reading her story. Indu, the protagonist feels the same way when a friend tells her about her writing: "If I hadn't known it was you who had written that story, I'd have thought it was a man" (79). Such assumptions of gender positions occur many times in the male and female writings. As for instance, Joyce's protean language, a characteristic of female language, masquerades his male identity. French feminist critics see this female potential in Joyce's use of instable and symbolic language.

A work of art may not be strictly autobiographical but a work of art, as it were, is also partly an unconscious mind's creation of the creator himself or herself. Deshpande may not be an autobiographical novelist in many of her novels but at times we see her quite inseparable from the emotional and psychological attitude and statements made by her characters. A writer's mind finds expression in the characters whether male or female. She or he may speak in the role of a woman or a man as the situation demands. One need not be strictly confined to one sex only. A woman writer may demand man's attention and vice-versa. Deshpande got so surprised when one of her stories was sent back by a publisher with a comment that it should be sent to a woman's magazine as if sex is attached so unalterably to a text. Sex has a free play in a given text, it is the mind of the artist that is there for the reader to see in the way he or she tries to. One can cite her statement from one of her interviews, "some of my thoughts are always there. They are there for the reader to pick and choose."[17] In *Moving On* too, the novelist seems to express her own views regarding the casual attitude towards women's writing through the character of the protagonist's father when he expresses his regret for not taking his wife's writing as seriously as he had regarded his professional writing. He thought writing for her was only a pastime, a kind of hobby. Now, after her death, he comes to know that she wrote not only fiction but also stories of women, about love, marriage and the home. His realization of the seriousness of her profession as a writer, though late, subtly conveys some message as he says, 'And if that wasn't trivial, what was it? So I thought. Now I think I should have respected what Vasu was doing. She belonged to a profession which deserved much more than the condescension I granted it' (201).

Shashi Deshpande is a very conscious and serious writer. She takes great care in choosing words to avoid any melodramatic statement and to have a kind of "subtlety of approach"[18]. She started her writing career late but she has learnt about language very seriously. She opines that craftsmanship is so important in writing and one can learn it only by doing. R.S. Pathak rightly states: "Deshpande's writings once again prove that art lies in concealing art. The highly functional language with telling economy that she uses is an important asset of hers as a fiction writer."[19]

Deshpande as a novelist lays emphasis more on characterization than on plots, as she says, "All my novels are like this: there is no plot, I only have the characters, characters with whom I live for years, about whom I know almost everything before I begin to tell their story."[20] For her, every novel starts with people and the novelist seems to agree with what Ivy Compton-Burnett states, "As regards plots I find real life no help at all. Real life seems to have no plots."[21] As far as technique is concerned, Deshpande takes a lot of concentration. What she tells Lakshmi Holmstrom is worth-citing: "Technique is something which I have to worry a lot about. I have to work at it and think about it and it takes me a long time to hit upon it exactly. It's like setting a tanpura, you know, before a concert begins."[22]

In the same interview, she admits candidly that she borrows the alternative uses of first person and third person narrative techniques from an American novelist, Lisa Alther. By employing such techniques, the novelist has gained the advantage of double perspective. She can capture the intensity of emotions and feelings of her characters using the first person narration for the past events and on the contrary, she shows an objective view using the third person narration while dealing with the present. Intermittently she uses the stream of consciousness technique to present the inner psyche of her protagonists sensitively. Besides, there are some alterations in her latest two novels in which she employs only the first person narrations by various characters other than the protagonists. For instance, she uses the voice of Jiji, the protagonist and her father (through his long, intimate diary, covering seven chapters, sharing his innermost thoughts and feelings as his days are numbered). In her latest novel, Deshpande's extensive use of letters deserves special attention. There are as many as twenty letters written by eight characters, covering more than forty pages. This extensive use of letters, in this age of computer and mobile, seems a little odd though writing letters as a means of communication by some seniors like Sindhu (the protagonist's aunt) and Janaradhan Rao (her grandfather's friend) is quite convincing, considering their age and circumstances. However, through this technique, the novelist is able to explore the inner thoughts, personal and subjective views of various characters on varied subjects, thereby adding variety to the narration.

She proves her excellence as a novelist by successfully employing recurrent metaphors and motifs. They include 'the dark' and 'the sunlight,' 'sleep' and 'dream,' 'house' and 'homecoming,' 'roots and shadows,' 'death' and 'life,' 'silences' and 'the binding vine.' Of all the motifs employed by her, silence dominates and becomes all pervading in all her novels. It plays a pivotal role in the lives of many of her characters, especially while dealing with the theme of alienation reflecting the realities of modern life. Most of the problems in human relationships arise owing to lack of communication. Silence becomes an essential part of life as stated by Saru in *The Dark Holds No Terrors* (35). It is perhaps silence or lack of communication between the husband and the wife that causes failure of their relationship once fulfilled and satisfied. The husband, Manohar, feels bad and humiliated when others directly or indirectly point out that his wife earns more and is more successful than he is. Then, he becomes a sadist in his attempt to assert his manhood. Saru, recalling this sad incident with regrets, feels:

> I should have spoken about it the very first day. But I didn't and each time it happens and I don't speak, I put another brick on the wall of silence between us.[23]

Again lack of communication between Saru and her mother makes their relationship very bitter.

In *That Long Silence*, as the title suggests, Jaya, the protagonist, undergoes a long silence throughout the novel, though it ends with a hope of erasing that silence. The treatment of silence by Deshpande is not merely a form of lack of communication, but it is a mode of reaction, protest. Women and only women are subjected to this kind of suffering when they are segregated from the male-made culture as evidenced when Jaya finds her name not included in the long list of names in the family tree, not even her aunties, mother and even her grandmother. To this she said nothing she "had learnt it at last—no questions, no retorts. Only silence" (143).

Another extreme case is Kalyani and Shripati, in *A Matter of Time* who lived in total silence for thirty-five years after they lost their only invalid son in a railway station for which the former was accused of having been responsible. Women take silence as a means of internalizing their suffering. One can just see Sumi's suffering in silence when her husband walked out of the family. Her enduring silence was so deep that even her daughters failed to understand it and hence, mistook it for indifference until the end of the novel. Gopal, the male protagonist, felt the emptiness of life as he says:

> Emptiness, I realized then, is always waiting for us . . . it's just deceiving ourselves when we say we are not alone. It is the desperation of a drowning person that makes us cling to other humans. All human ties are only a masquerade. Some day, some time, the pretence fails us and we have to face the truth. (52)

In *The Binding Vine*, Urmila witnessed the long silence of Akka, of Meera, of Shakutai's sister, of Kalpana who was in coma and many others like them. Thus many characters in feminist fiction assume 'silence' as an indispensable part of it. Because of the long suppression, women tend to be mute and silent. They remained voiceless, unheard of, turned out at the margin. It becomes a mask of suffering, pain, and also a feminist strategy to withdraw to female self with a measure of silent communication without speech and language. It is the language of protest and suffering. In the novel in question, Mohan's mother's struggle was "so bitter that silence was the only weapon. Silence and surrender" (36). The theme of alienation and loneliness is also there in *Roots and Shadows.* Indu, the protagonist, says:

> I had pulled in my boundaries and found myself the poorer for it. Alienation, I know now, is not the answer. On the contrary too much of it and we can die of a terrible loneliness of the spirit. 'I am alone.' . . . they seem to me to be the most poignant words in any language.[24]

In the novel, *In the Country of Deceit*, silence is used in two ways, serving both negative and positive purposes. Devayani found Ashok's silence 'impenetrable' on certain subjects, blocking their communication. On the other hand, when they're together, sometimes, they lay in silence just to enjoy each other's company. Sometimes silence is used as a means of communication as she says, "No more conversations, not even monosyllabic answers. Even a 'yes' or a 'no' can give you away. Why even a silence can give you away!" (78)

Another theme that pervades most of her novels is the theme of death followed by emptiness. It is Aditya's untimely death in

Small Remedies that has left Madhu completely grief-stricken and devastated. Similarly, it is the death of her only son, Dhruva, in *The Dark Holds No Terrors* that unfolds Saru's mother's distress. Urmila suffers the death of her baby daughter in *The Binding Vine*. In her recent novel, *Moving On* one finds death staring characters in the face. There are so many deaths in the novel and the novelist is at her best in expressing the emptiness and the loneliness that generally accompany the death of near and dear ones as felt by Jiji's father when his wife died:

> I woke up in the morning after Vasu's death to a sense of emptiness, as if I was in an empty house. I woke up to a sense of void which was *within* me. The house was neither empty nor silent. . . . But the sounds seemed distant; it was as if I was enclosed in a vacuum and nothing could reach me. [25]

After the death of his brother, R.K., B.K. becomes a sad and lonely man. Jiji who was intimately attached to her younger sister Malu and her husband was struck with shock when the two died. Their death was a personal loss to her as if she had lost her partner and part of her self and soul.

> And there's Malu, Malu whose death left an aching emptiness inside me. Shyam's death devastated me, for Shyam was my lover, he was my companion. In losing him, I became a woman without a partner. But Malu was a part of me, she was connected to my being, my soul. When she died, it was like losing something of my own self. I felt the way Mai must have done after they amputated her leg. Incomplete. (327)

The theme of 'life and death' is very much a part of Deshpande's fiction. For instance, Sumi, the protagonist in *A Matter of Time*, died in an accident when she was ready to face life and the world with a new hope after having struggled for long. In the same way, Rani (Devayani or Devi's friend), the former actress, met with a car accident and had serious injuries, destroying her hope of making a comeback in a dream project. When Deshpande was asked the reason of such untimely death and unexpected accident, she stated that 'death' and 'accident' happen in real life and she is reflecting that aspect of reality. Most of the philosophy of 'death' and 'accident' comes from Sindhu being a cancer patient:

> I've accepted my illness, my possible death, as a matter of fact. It didn't come easy, let me tell you that. To overcome your fear of death, you have to move from 'the world ends with me' to 'the world goes on without me.' It is a great leap, the biggest step a human can take. (20)

Devayani's father committed suicide 'unable to bear heavy burden of life imposed upon him from an early age. Loneliness and alienation are also very much part of modern life. Both Devayani's father and Jiji's husband Shyam in *Moving On* suffered from alienation of self and society before meeting their tragic end.

Recurring dreams is another motif frequently used by the novelist. Devayani or Devi in the novel, *In the Country of Deceit*, like Saru in *The Dark Holds No Terrors*, was haunted by some kind of dreams in which a powerful man came to her, 'the man standing at the edge of the grove of trees, his face in the shadows.' (94) She knew what he wanted, she wanted to run but she couldn't, reflecting one of her childhood incidents when she along with her girl friends was threatened by the watchman in the mango orchard. Since then she had been having the same nightmare. As the novel progresses, she was no longer afraid of the man when she met Ashok and finally she could overcome her fear of man.

The novelist's use of symbol and metaphor is worth mentioning. In *Roots and Shadows,* the old house stands for tradition and old values, a symbol of authority as Indu says, 'Yes the house had been a trap too, binding me to a past I had to move away from (204).' Everyone is bound by the strict authority and discipline of Akka, Indu's aunt, a rich widow. After her death, Indu has decided to sell the house, and this is symbolic of her freedom and self-assertion, defying the old authority. By doing so she feels 'as if she had cut away all the unnecessary, uneven edges of me (204). At the very outset of the novel, *In the Country of Deceit,* the picture of the demolition of the old house is presented. which is soon replaced by a new house, 'a complete reversal of the old house' (4). The drastic change is used as a metaphor in Devayani's life which would take a sudden turn in her boring life. When she moves into the new house, Devayani feels both physically and mentally free for the first time with no one to look after and take care of. She has changed drastically after she met Ashok as observed by others, 'from a dull uninteresting old-fashioned Devi' to 'a beautiful woman with her own unique style. . . . As if someone has brought out the shine and polish in' her (148). The changes and development in a small town, Rajnur also serves as a metaphor to the protagonist's life. From a not-so-happening small town, Rajnur became a fast developing town with new educational institutions, professional colleges, shopping complexes, restaurants, dhabas, bank, cyber cafes, a post-office—all the requirements of a modern town. This parallel development in the personality of the protagonist and physical changes in Rajnur is beautifully intertwined.

Another interesting aspect upon which the novelist draws very efficiently is the constant reference to myths, especially to the great epics of India—the *Mahabharata* and the *Ramayana* and to popular folktales. Deshpande not only uses these myths and folktales by simply referring to them but also provides us with a different reading, a new insight and perspective by shifting the focus from the male-centre to the female perspective. Most of the myths and folktales that had been constructed to the advantage of men have been dismantled and deconstructed. Women in the great epics were made just as tools for benefitting man. Carolyne Larrington has made the right observation: "Women's problems in general feature little in the main line of the epic, which by and large is not concerned with women's feelings except where they have repercussions on the male-dominated storyline."[26]

This very fact is what Deshpande is trying to juxtapose with the way she reviews them in her writings. In the story, "The Inner Rooms,"[27] Amba is seen in the limelight and Bhishma, the most revered personality of the great epic, *The Mahabharata*, perhaps, for the first time, is on the periphery. Bhishma had ruined her life and in her rage, she promised to kill him. Her anger was shown as unwomanly but Deshpande, through the character of Sumi, makes her the heroine who fights for her right and life; even Supranakha (the sister of Ravana) who had been treated as a wanton woman when she made advances to Lakshman is hailed as "a woman charged with sexuality, not frightened of displaying it" (*A Matter of Time*, 191). In the story "The Day of the Golden Deer,"[28] we can see the feelings and emotions, anger and rage of Sita when she heard the orders of Rama.

Such themes, besides being framed feminist or women oriented, can cast Indianness in fiction as distinctively rooted in national consciousness and Indian tradition. There is reference to the epic *Mahabharata* in *In the Country of Deceit,* relating the story of Devayani—'the reckless, arrogant, stupid girl who thought that her father's position would get her what she wanted. Who fell in love, twice, with men who didn't want her and married the second man, a king, against his wishes' (36). Devayani, the protagonist, had no sympathy for the 'stupid girl' who made her rival, the princess her slave and took her to her new home. The woman she hated most, whom she had wanted to humiliate became her 'husband's dearly loved mistress' (36). Though she was the queen, the other woman, Sharmishta had the king and a son, Puru who became a king after his father. The protagonist didn't like her name to be associated with this woman 'who never got what she wanted, who never understood what love meant' (6) Deshpande's use of this story seemed to have a significant effect on the life of the protagonist. It appears that she unconsciously tries to distance herself from the Devayani of the *Mahabharata*, and the fact that the latter didn't have or find any love in her life might have haunted her with the fear that she too was destined to be barren of love in her own life. Deshpande relates the story of Krishna and Sudama to Saru's coming back to her parental home after a long time in *The Dark Holds No Terrors*. In the same novel, she brings in the story of Dhruva with slight modification to the sibling rivalry over parental love and affection. In *The Binding Vine*, through Mira's poems, the novelist refers to the story of Laxmi and Narayan:

> But tell me, friend, did Laxmi too
> twist brocade tassels round her fingers
> and tremble, fearing the coming
> of the dark-clouded, engulfing night? (66)

Here, she seems to ask if Luxmi too, like any other ordinary female, trembles with fear of the dark, engulfing night. It makes us ask ourselves if male domination and female subjugation are also there among gods and goddesses. Jaya in *That Long Silence* compares herself with Gandhari who had bandaged her eyes to become blind like her husband, and in the similar manner Jaya had to follow her husband blindly, himself going into hiding following a business malpractice. We can hear the sincere voice of Kunti in the story, "Hear me Sanjaya,"[29] of Sita in "The Day of the Golden Deer," of Draupadi in "And What Has Been Decided."[30] Thus Deshpande is adept at using the mythical women characters while highlighting the imprisoning effects of modern life brought by men over women. Through this method, voices have finally found their outlets after so many ages of suppression.

Parent-child hatred is another theme that often snowballs into significance in Deshpande's novels. Through the discreet exploitation of the myths of Shiva, Gauri and their son, Shashi Deshpande deals with the love-hate relationship between father and son. In the story, Gauri, wife of Shiva, produced a son out of the sweat of her body so that he could guard her, standing at the door, while she was taking bath. When Shiva returned home, the child confronted him. Shiva killed him by cutting off his head. To please Gauri, he put on the body the head of an elephant, which had been sleeping with its head to the north. Such father-son hatred theme is prevalent in *That Long Silence*. Justifying the conflict Jaya says, "After all, every son must fight his father to prove himself, every daughter her mother" (9). In *The Dark Holds No Terrors,* Madhav said that he hated his father since his father saw only himself and others did not exist in his world. Saru asked herself if it's always that way—fathers and sons, mothers and daughters. Renu and she; Abi and his father (151). In the same novel, Saru and her mother, as mentioned earlier, had a bitter relationship, hating each other to the extent that her mother even at the moment of dying denied the existence of her daughter. Her motherly love and affection was kept preserved for her son, Dhruva who died by drowning.

Mother-daughter conflict again appears in *The Binding Vine* when Vanaa confided to Urmila that her daughter, Mandira hated her but not her husband. This is true in the lower section too. Kalpana hated her mother who sacrificed everything for the family. She blamed her mother when her father left them for another woman. She gave money to her father more readily though she knew that he would use it for gambling but she grumbled when her mother asked for it to use for the family. In *Small Remedies*, Madhu's obsessive love for her son may be just a small example. Attention towards opposite sex is evident in the same novel where Munni, the only daughter of Savitri Bai Indorekar, rejected her mother throughout her life and chose to long for the father whom she had hardly seen. In *Moving On*, Jiji and her mother and later on, herself and her daughter, Sachi do not get along, and 'Raja and his father could not get on with each other. A classic father-son relationship' (90). In the novel, *In the Country of Deceit*, Sindhu, Devi's aunt, was accused of being an uncaring mother by her daughter, Tara, misunderstanding her principle of non-interference to her grown up children as negligence by saying that she 'was not like other mothers' and she was 'unnatural' (117). Such relationships take on the colouring of Oedipus complex or the opposite, however though such a point is never so alarmingly explicit as in Lawrence's *Sons and Lovers*.

Deshpande has an eye for popular folktales with the intention of laying emphasis on a certain point in context. Her reflection on such scenes is meaningful. In *The Dark Holds No Terrors* there is an allusion to a Sanskrit story about a woman who would not disturb her husband's sleep even at the cost of her child who would have been dead by fire had not Agni, the god of fire, himself come and saved the child of this "blessed woman" (207). The irony implied is more pronounced, when the novelist speaks through the mouth of Saru:

> Now she thought . . . who wrote that story? A man, of course. Telling all women for all time . . . your duty to me comes first. And women, poor fools, believed him. (207)

In *That Long Silence*, there is the story of "the foolish, improvident, irresponsible, gullible crow;" and "the cautions, self-centred, worldly-wise, dutiful shrewd sparrow" (17). The foolish crow built his house of dung, and the wise sparrow built of wax. In the rainy season the crow's nest was washed away. So, he pleaded the sparrow to let him in. The cunning sparrow, after making him wait for a long time, finally let the crow in and told him to warm himself on the frying pan and the poor crow died. No doubt, the story gives picture of a clever sparrow which derived sadistic pleasure from the situation. But the message it offers in a feminist text is that a married housewife needs to be ruthless, exact and unmindful of what others expect of her. This corresponds to the new role and status of Suhasini, the post-marriage name of Jaya, given by her husband, and rereading of Deshpande's use of folktales and folksongs is not always aimed at extolling female virtues in male constructed stories. She either reinterprets them or questions them. In her essay "Of Kitchens and Goddesses," reference to a Bengali folksong, "If you serve milk and rice to everyone and content yourself with plain rice alone/we shall be able to say you are the proper/daughter of a wise father" [30] is just to question and not to accept the culturally given woman nature which is made a qualification for a woman's socialization and acceptability in a given society.

In course of time, such folksongs and folktales condition the inner psyche of both men and women in such a way that any sacrifice made by women seems to be quite normal. For instance, the above song exemplifies the point that women have been serving men's wish at their cost. One can see when women are fasting, they are not exempted from cooking an entire meal for the rest of the family who are not fasting. Deshpande seems to have a strong message against such self-deprivation. Saru, in *The Dark Holds No Terrors* reflects the views of the novelist when she thinks of these women as

> stupid, silly martyrs . . . ; idiotic heroines. Going on with their tasks, and destroying themselves in the bargain, for nothing, but a meaningless modesty. Their unconscious, unmeaning heroism, born out of the myth of self-sacrificing martyred woman, did not arouse either her pity or her admiration. It made her angry. (107)

As pointed out earlier, for Deshpande, literary text is a means of protest, the characters bear the stamp of the social norms as a reaction to and against such forms as presented by the culture in question in this regard. With this she enacts and relates the past to the present and vice versa. In this connection what she says of the importance of the myths to Lakshmi Holmstrom is relevant:

> we relate a great deal of our personal lives, our daily lives, to the myths. We find parallels as matter of course. . . . I'm interested, I think, with what we do with our past as well as what our past does to us.[32]

Shashi Deshpande's novels continue to have quite similar themes and characters. Almost all her protagonists are educated and working, middle class, married for more than fifteen years with one or two children, with the exception of Devi aged twenty-six, not yet married. They are not happy in their married life because of varied reasons. However, generally speaking, they suffer because they act like puppets, much against their modern outlook. The novelist provides some circumstances, for instance, death of a child, death of a family member, coming back to their parental home or a situation which give them opportunity to look into their life and their problems as they are away from their normal routine life. They exile themselves in their self-created shell, recalling and examining each and every little detail of their past life. In the process, they have a chance to look at their own life from a distance. It enables them to look at the problems objectively. They analyze the root cause of their problems and sufferings, and finally they are able to come out with certain realization. They realize that they were not aware that life offered them more than one chance but that very fact remained oblivious to them. Jaya, at the end of the novel, realizes, "I've always thought—there's only one life, no chance of a reprieve, no second chances. But in this life itself there are so many crossroads, so many choices" (191-92).

Shashi Deshpande is a modern woman writer who writes with commitment and consciousness of women's life and their problems. Her treatment of and dealings with her women characters clearly show that she writes drawing upon her experience as a woman. Women's authentic and sincere voice is what the novelist attempts to bring forth. Most of her protagonists suffer from identity crisis at some point of their lives and hence, their struggle to search for their identities becomes the main concern of her novels. Ultimately they are able to discover their true self. Deshpande as a novelist may be placed in the third phase in the history of women writers as divided by Elaine Showalter. Women writers are grouped into three phases—the "Feminine phase" (1840-1880), the "Feminist phase" (1880-1920), the "Female phase" (1920-present). According to Showalter, the "Feminine phase" is the "phase of *imitation* of the prevailing modes of dominant tradition, and *internalization* of its standard of art and its views on social roles."[33] In this period, both the production and consumption of literature were considered exclusively as males' domain. No wonder some women writers like George Eliot wrote under male pseudonyms. The second phase, the "Feminist phase" is marked by "*protest* against these standards and values, and advocacy of minority rights and values, including a demand for autonomy."[34] Finally, there is "Female phase" of "*self-discovery*, a turning inward freed from some of the dependency of opposition, a search for identity."[35] Deshpande would be properly and adequately fitted into the "Female phase" not only because she chronologically falls within this period but also because of her very commitment and preoccupation. She is not one who tries "to fit women between the lines of the male tradition"; but rather she "focuses on the newly visible world of female culture."[36] Right from her very first novel, *The Dark Holds No Terrors*, to the latest one, the novelist's depiction of her women characters and their problems reveals her consciousness of the multi-layered sexual politics prevailing in the society through the ages. She neither imitates the masculine mode of writing nor does she blindly follow the militant feminist writers. This means that she writes not what she must but what she chooses, and as a very sensitive feminist writer, she knows the huge gap between men's world and women's world and wishes to bridge the two worlds so as to create a harmonious society of both man and woman.

Interestingly Deshpande's novels have typical endings. They end with an optimistic note and hope not for just survival but for living a meaningful life. Unlike Anita Desai's neurotic, psychic and suicidal heroines like Maya in *Cry, the Peacock*, Deshpande's protagonists strive to find a balance, a way of finding some solution to their problems and sufferings. In this sense, it would not be wrong to say that her novels are positive in attitude towards women's life and their problems. Here, the novelist seems to agree with what Elaine Showalter says: "women's literature must go beyond these scenarios of compromise, madness and death. Although the reclamation of suffering is the beginning, its purpose is to discover the new world."[37] They are ready to rectify their fault for a better life and even go on accepting things beyond expectation. They had turned their back to their problems and silently endured with constant fear, but they at the very end of the novels are sure of themselves and ready to face anything in life.

Another important aspect of Deshpande as a novelist is her sympathetic treatment of her male characters, though she does not focus on them as she does on her women characters. She can reach out to the suffering and pain that is there in the mind of her male characters too. In *A Matter of Time*, the treatment of the male character, Gopal is noteworthy. Here, the novelist successfully presents the inner working of his psyche as sympathetic as she deals with her female characters. Though Gopal's desertion of his family abruptly for the reasons not known to himself even, seems to be cruel, her insightful observation and objective treatment of the character makes it possible to win our sympathy towards him. Deshpande, who has so far used female protagonists, for the first time, uses a male protagonist through the character of Gopal. In her novel, *Moving On,* Shashi Deshpande marvellously relives another male protagonist as the diary entries are unravelled. Here the novelist, quite successfully, expresses the very intimate feelings and sentiments of a dying, old man, looking at his life from the very beginning.

Deshpande's male characters as found in her earlier novels do not share the same space like their female counterparts but the novelist's realistic and sympathetic treatment of male characters is noteworthy. Devayani's father was shown as a failure, burdened with financial problems. Being the oldest son of an irresponsible father, he had to look after his younger siblings' education, to take care of her sisters' marriage. When he married Pushpa, a rich man's daughter, everyone thought he married for money but it wasn't true. At the age of forty, he gave up a good job in his father-in-law's bank. 'Maybe he wanted to get away from being Krishna Bhat's son-in-law,' or perhaps 'he was tired of family responsibilities' (60). He had his own dreams of plantation that couldn't be fulfilled. He suffered from depression, midlife crisis. At last, he committed suicide. Towards the end of the novel, when Devayani was bedridden after an accident, she was able to understand her father, the darkness he was in and 'the despair that had driven him to his death' (249). Deshpande also projects him as the victim of male's ego reflecting our society's pressure on individual male. The patriarchal society demands some expected role not only from women but also from men to act in a certain way. Men are always expected to be superior, stronger and bread-earner. Devayani's father did not touch a single penny from his wife's money to pay the heavy family debt and even for their daughter's marriage, all because it would hurt his male ego.

Other male characters like Shree, Devayani's brother-in-law (they grew up together in the same colony), Iqbal, her lawyer (for a dispute over land) and Keshavrao, her uncle, were depicted as understanding and sympathetic persons. They too, in their own way reached out to Devayani to lend a helping hand. It was Shree and Keshav who wrote to her, trying to reason the consequences of her relationship with a married man. Finally it was Iqbal who offered her much needed work as his assistant, helping her to cope up with her life after Ashok. Through these characters, Deshpande seems to suggest the possibility of male-female bonding and its positive result in the individual's life.

DSP Ashok Chinnappa was a man living for the moment, doing well in his career as policeman but seemed to have not-so-good married life because of which he had many women in his life. However he had perhaps found something special in Devayani, a feeling he never had before, when he first saw her. He was depicted as one who asserted himself and knew the world around him but because of his loving daughter, he was ready to face unhappy married life, sacrificing his undying love for Devayani. This shows that men too, like women in Indian society, had to give up their individual likes for the sake of the family. In their last meeting, he said, 'I'm sorry, Divya, I am sorry. I can't lose my daughter, I can't let her lose me' (299).

It does not seem that the novelist uses the male protagonists just to show her competence to explore the other gender's consciousness but to reveal the dreams, the uncertainties and the inner psyche of the male characters more convincingly. In doing so, Shashi Deshpande is at her best. Jasbir Jain rightly observes, "when a woman writer works her narrative through a male consciousness, questions of sexuality and psychology are raised" but "No eye-brows were raised when Samuel Richardson wrote first *Pamela*."[38] In the same essay, the observation she made deserves some mention:

> Women writers when they turn to male narrators are not necessarily guided by the desire to escape a female consciousness or to demonstrate that they have a grasp over the male psyche. Most of the time, it is not the average swash-buckling hero who interests them. What fascinate them are the dreams men have and the layers of sensitivity which lies undiscovered in them.[39]

While dealing with the suffering lot of women in a male-dominated society, Deshpande is careful enough not to miss out the female domination and its effects on the lives of men. Deshpande acknowledges that there is female domination in our society as much as male domination. What she tells Lakshmi Holmstrom in an interview may be cited:

> To me it is very important, the power that women wield as well as the power that men possess. It's much a part of what I want to say. In *That Long Silence*, for example, there is the power that Ajji has over her sons, over Jaya's father. He has to go and see her every day. Jaya says, "How is it I never noticed it before, the power of women?"[40]

Saru, in *The Dark Holds No Terrors* says that she feels pity for her husband as she realizes that he is groping in the dark as much as she is. We find Saru's mother dominating her father.

In *Roots and Shadows* too, 'Akka,' Indu's grandmother who was a rich childless widow, came back to her brother's house and maintained an absolute control over the family. This aspect shows how truthfully Deshpande maintains impartiality towards both her male and female characters, a characteristic rarely found in contemporary novelists. Her insight into seeing things or characters or situations objectively makes her writing realistic. This may be one reason why we often find difficulties in finding out who is the victim and who the predator. Often the same person appears to be both. Sarita, for instance, appears to be the victim of her husband's nightmarish brutality on bed. She, later, realized that she had been overwhelmed by the attention and regard her recent success had given to her and that she had neglected and ignored the feelings and sentiments of her husband. She was too involved and busy in her career that she never cared to give a thought to finding out the root cause of her husband's sudden change of behaviour towards her. If she cared and tried, perhaps, she could have saved their marriage in time. Her indifference made the matters worse by turning Manohar into a sadist. On the other hand, Manohar who seems to be the predator turns out to be a victim of male's ego constructed by the so-called patriarchal society. It is an irony that the very norms once formed of the males, for the males and by the males attack them and make them victims of their own making.

One of the reasons why Shashi Deshpande, in spite of her literary talent, does not get wide recognition and acclamation especially abroad, as compared with some of her contemporaries such as Anita Desai may be because she writes independently without being conscious of what her readers, specially, the Western readers expect from Indian literature. She neither uses 'Indianism' nor does she try to simplify certain concepts, ideas, culture and myths purely Indian. What she tells M.D. Riti in an interview "There is No Looking Back" is quite ambivalent. She is neither there nor here as it were:

> I do not use Indianism to make my writing look Indian. I never try to make India look exotic. I do not think of a Western audience at all. I belong to Indian literature. I would not like ever to be called an Indo-Anglican writer. I feel strongly about that.[41]

It seems she is rather backward in her conviction and commitment that to be an Indo-Anglican writer is so by virtue of one's adherence to the social, cultural ethos and reality. Maybe because of this reason why some German students said that they found the character of Sumi in *A Matter of Time* puzzling as she did not conform to their idea of an Indian woman. According to the critic Meenakshi Mukherjee: "her special valued [sic] lies in an uncompromising toughness, in her attempts to do what has never been attempted in English, her insistence on being read on her own terms and a refusal to be packaged according to the demands of the market."[42]

As discussed before, Deshpande does not like to conform to any kind of categorization or labeling. She has declared herself a feminist but she has been defending herself from being called a feminist writer. Whether or not she is a feminist writer, her fiction certainly contains some basic feminist elements, though there are also many other elements, which are not feminist in orientation. Her method and vision as a woman writer is different from that of the Western feminist writers or even her contemporary Indian feminist writers. Her fiction shows a clear departure from the male writing tradition, which itself is a qualification for feminist writing. Each of her novels is a journey of self-discovery, self-realization and self-actualization. She is one of those writers/novelists writing about women's problems and predicaments but that does not necessarily mean that she is always woman-centred with a predetermined bias that all women are wronged and men an instrument of female oppression and suffering. For all that women suffer, man need not be always blamed because women's sins are mostly created by themselves. All the more women need to be conscious of their own role and responsibility in the society. Women are to reform themselves as much as men are to be reformed. Looked at from this angle what Deshpande argues is in favour of a balanced society where man and woman share equally, understand each other on an equal footing. That perhaps will be able to remove sexual and gender disparity. Deshpande, the novelist, will have to be seen in this light for proper investigation and interrogation. Her feminism bears a totally different stamp. Feminist, yes, she is one but with a difference—that is to be established when Deshpande's work needs to be properly construed.

NOTES

1. Helene Cixous, "The Laugh of the Medusa," trans. Keith Cohen and Paula Cohen, Mary Eagleton, ed., *Feminist Literary Theory: A Reader* (Rpt. Massachusetts: Blackwell, 1996), 320.
2. Vanamala Vishwanath, "A Woman's World . . . All the Way!" (Interview), R.S. Pathak, ed. *The Fiction of Shashi Deshpande*, 235.
3. R.S. Pathak, "Shashi Deshpande and the Woman Question" *Modern Indian Novels in English* (Delhi: Saujanya, 1999), 204.
4. S. Prasanna Sree, "An Interview with Shashi Deshpande," Amarnath Prasad, ed., *New Lights on Indian Women Novelists in English* (Delhi: Saujanya, 2003), 96.
5. *Ibid.*, 93.
6. Qtd. R.S. Pathak, "The Making of the Novelist," R.S. Pathak, ed., *The Fiction of Shashi Deshpande*, 18.
7. S. Prasanna Sree, 94.
8. Shashi Deshpande, "Writing from the Margin," *Writing from the Margin and Other Essays* (New Delhi: Penguin, 2003), 161.
9. Qtd. Kavita Sinha, "Women," *Telegraph*, III, Sunday, 6 Oct. 2002.
10. Sujata Sankranti, "No Identity No Self!" Meenakshi Bharat, ed., *Desert in Bloom: Contemporary Indian Women's Fiction in English* (Delhi: Pencraft International, 2004), 223.
11. Shashi Deshpande, "Where Do We Belong?" *Writing from the Margin and Other Essays*, 53.
12. Mrinalini Sebastian, *The Novels of Shashi Deshpande in Postcolonial Arguments* (New Delhi: Prestige, 2000), 220.
13. M. Mani Meitei, *The Stream of Consciousness Techniques with Special Reference to the Novels of Virginia Woolf* Diss., Manipur University, 1987, 100.
14. Vanamala Vishwanath, 236.
15. Shashi Deshpande, *The Binding Vine* (Rpt. New Delhi: Penguin, 2001), 76.
16. Shashi Deshpande, "The Dilemma of the Woman Writer," R.S. Pathak, ed., *The Fiction of Shashi Deshpande.*

17. Geetha Gangadharan, "Denying the Otherness" (interview), R.S. Pathak, ed. *The Fiction of Shashi Deshpande*, 253.
18. Lakshmi Holmstrom, "Shashi Deshpande Talks to Lakshmi Holmstrom," R.S. Pathak, ed., *The Fiction of Shashi Deshpande*, 242.
19. R.S. Pathak, "Shashi Deshpande: The Making of the Novelist," *The Fiction of Shashi Deshpande*, 26.
20. Shashi Deshpande, "In First Person," *Writing from the Margin and Other Essays*, 19.
21. Miriam Allott, *Novelists on the Novels* (London: Routledge and Kegan Paul C., 1959), 249.
22. Lakshmi Holmstrom, 248.
23. Shashi Deshpande, *The Dark Holds No Terrors* (Rpt. New Delhi: Penguin, 1990), 96.
24. Shashi Deshpande, *Roots and Shadows* (New Delhi: Disha, 1992), 10.
25. Shashi Deshpande, *Moving On* (New Delhi: Penguin, 2004), 111.
26. Carolyne Larrington, ed., *The Women's Companion to Mythology* (London: Harper Collins, 1992), 209.
27. Shashi Deshpande, "The Inner Rooms," *The Intrusion and Other Stories* (New Delhi: Penguin), 1993.
28. "The Day of the Golden Deer," *Collected Stories*, Vol. 2. (New Delhi: Penguin India, 2004).
29. "Hear me, Sanjaya . . .," *Collected Stories*, Vol. 2.
30. "And What Has Been Decided," *Collected Stories*, Vol. 2.
31. "Of Kitchens and Goddesses" *Writing from the Margin and Other Essays*, 141.
32. Lakshmi Holmstrom, 246 and248.
33. Elaine Showalter, "A Literature of Their Own: British Women Novelists from Bronte to Lessing," Mary Eagleton, ed., *Feminist Literary Theory: A Reader*, 15-16.
34. *Ibid.*, 16.
35. *Ibid.*
36. Elaine Showalter, "Toward a Feminist Poetics," Mary Jacobus, ed., *Women Writing and Writing about Women* (New York: Barns and Noble, 1979), 28.
37. *Ibid.*, 39.
38. Jasbir Jain, "Men in the Minds of Women: Women Writers and Male Narrators in the Fiction of Nayantara Sahgal, Anita Desai and Githa Hariharan," Meenakshi Bharat, ed., *Desert in Bloom: Contemporary*

Indian Women's Fiction in English (Dehli: Pencraft International, 2004), 4.

39. *Ibid.*, 57.
40. Lakshmi Holmstrom, 244.
41. M.D. Riti, "There's No Looking Back" (interview) R.S. Pathak, ed., *The Fiction of Shashi Deshpande*, 240.
42. Meenakshi Mukherjee, 21 Feb 2006 < http: // www.Indiaclub. Com /Fiction/Moving On/Review/2>.

Feminism: An Overview

Feminism is a social, political and literary movement that strives to discard all forms of domination and unequal treatment of women so as to bring a well-balanced and harmonious society. It advocates the right of women as individuals. It opposes all forms of relegation of women to the margin, and aims at reforming the existing social structure that enhances male supremacy and female domination. It is much against categorization and marginalization of women as 'other' or 'second sex.' It is unquestionably 'pro-women' as against the male formed ideas and social constructs. It works for the betterment and improvement of the present lot and condition of women. Feminism encompasses and involves all female/woman concerned social and political issues and literary production that would contribute to the representation of women on a par with man. Feminism, thus, is many faceted and pluralistic in approach. Because of its very complex, dynamic nature there has not been a commonly accepted definition of Feminism. The definition varies because it is defined in different ways by different critics of varied interests and predilections and training. However, some of the definitions may be given. Alice Jardine defines feminism as a "movement from the point of view of, by, and for women."[1] In her discussion of Virginia Woolf, Herbert Marder says feminism is an "intense awareness" of woman's "identity as a woman, her interest in feminine problems."[2]

The question is why women need an identity of their own—the gendered identity. It is gender that divides man from woman, and this biological fact has been used for the exploitation of women by man in patriarchal society. Sexual and gender differentiation leads to women oppression and subjugation in male-dominated society or culture for generations thereby creating a history of women based on suffering, exploitation, lack of opportunities that in turn cause social and psychological disorders to women. This social and cultural construct of binary opposition on sexual lines needed to be challenged by women in terms of equal treatment of the sexes, equal rights, equal opportunities, sexual rights including the use of contraceptives, control over female body by women, even choice of motherhood—all implying women's self-determination in all spheres of life—social, political, economic (which means women's economic self-reliance not depending on man) and sexual. Feminists are/were concerned with these aspects, and they started fighting against disparity and injustice done to them by men through ages. Feminism, therefore, is a political movement aiming at women's self-consciousness, again through education, which would remove all prejudices against women. A feminist in essence is one who speaks of female cause. In this connection what Rebecca West writes is important to note:

> I myself have never been able to find out precisely what feminism is. I only know that people call me a feminist whenever I express sentiments about women that differentiate me from a doormat or a prostitute. But all Feminists share a commitment to, and enjoyment of, a woman-centred perspective. [3]

The term 'feminism' was first coined by Alexander Dumas, the French novelist of the nineteenth century, to refer to the women's liberation movement of that time, though it was mostly confined to political rights. Gradually it spread all over the world with almost all the aspects, including social, economic, educational, cultural and even religious, literary and psychological. People, especially women, began to question the existing systems that had separate code for men and women always to the disadvantages of the latter. Though feminism became more pronounced in the 19th and 20th centuries, French feminism traced back to the 14th century and identified Christaine de Pisan as the first modern feminist thinker as John Kelly says: "If Petrarch can be called the first modern man, then Christine de Pisan, the poet and author who introduced her countrymen Petrarch and Boccaccio, to Parisian culture in the early 1400, is surely the first modern woman."[4]

There were many pro-women writers following her but the early feminists did not have any definite term to name themselves. They shared certain outlook and vision that opposed the existing oppressive system. They were against the dominant culture of patriarchy. They defended women through their writings against various attacks and argued against those social and cultural constraints imposed on women in the society. These women formed a social group and jointly opposed the injustice, prejudices and misogyny. Women of all classes, including those aristocrat women realized the declining status of women day by day as compared to the status of men of their own classes. They became aware that perhaps their suffering was due to the sexual inequalities existing in the society.

Towards the second quarter of the 17th century, many radial English sects supported religious equality for women. Taking this opportunity, there were women who tried to liberate themselves from the clerical authority of male. "These women, like Anne Hutchinson, were 'feminists in action,' rather than theorists. Instead of elaborating their ideas in writing, they used them to modify or organize social forms in which women might be free of male power and authority over them."[5] These women were mostly educated who were fortunate enough to have education in a society where women were strictly forbidden for the same.

The awareness of the subjugation of women under the dominant culture of men spread its wings to other aspects too. After religious equality, the feminists of the 19th and 20th centuries fought for equal political rights. Eminent personalities like Mary Wollstonecraft (1750-1797) and John Stuart Mill (1806-1873) were the forerunners of the political emancipation of women. The Seneca Falls Declaration of Sentiments and Resolutions signed at the Seneca Falls, New York, in the year 1848 gave women the much-needed platform from where they organized themselves in a group and demanded women's political right. Their century-old struggle was finally rewarded when they won right to vote in England in the year 1918 and America in 1920. Many people had thought that with the attainment of political rights, women would be fully emancipated. Unfortunately, that was not the case as women were still subjected to other forms of male domination. Though the franchise failed to eradicate the social, economic and cultural inequalities existing in the society, it became an inspiring impetus of the future feminist movement.

As the movement continued and progressed, women became aware of all the inequalities and injustices in every walk of their everyday life and hence included many other aspects too. They no longer were content with the secondary position and the status of 'otherness' to their male counterparts. They wanted to eliminate all existing disparities and inequalities between the sexes. They challenged the social and economic injustices that maimed them. With the advent of the Industrial Revolution, women began to participate in the production process. Many men were not happy with the participation of women. They felt threatened since women would do the same amount of work for lower wages. It is ironically a sad situation while men never question their rights and positions in the society as if these come to them naturally and they resist and try every means to subdue every single independent move of women. This new breed of women stiffly challenged this kind of monopoly and hegemony exercised by men at the cost of women.

Women, all over the world, were greatly affected by the two Great World Wars and so many local wars like they had been affected by various Revolutions before. All of a sudden, they were exposed to the outside happenings and their lives were no longer confined to the four domestic walls. The movement revived as an important force especially in the Western countries by late 1960s. When women were protesting against the Vietnam War and fighting for the abolition of slavery as active members of the Civil Rights Movement, they began to notice the sexist attitude of their male colleagues. Soon, they realized that the 'modus operandi' used to enslave the Blacks was analogous to the oppressive system operated to relegate them. This realization awakened them and made them feel the need to form women as a separate group and struggled against any kind of injustice and inequality existing in the society, be it racism, sexism, capitalism or patriarchism. There has been no stopping since then.

It is difficult to say whether the earlier feminism influenced literature or literature influenced feminism but they influence each other a great deal. The writings of pro-women writers starting from Christine de Pisan to Mary Wollstonecraft greatly influenced the thinking and actions of the society. Books like *A Vindication of the Rights of Women* (1792) by Mary Wollstonecraft and *The Subjection of Women* (1869) by John Stuart Mill, were able to arouse and provoke violent responses, and also aroused consciousness to the existing social and economic injustices. These books drew the attention of the public to the need to re-establish a new society based on equality of men and women as pointed out by John Stuart Mill: "that the principle which relegates the existing social relations between the two sexes—the legal subordination of one sex to the other—is wrong in itself, and now one of the chief hindrances to human improvement; and that it ought to be replaced by a principle of perfect equality, admitting no power or privilege on the one side, or disability on the other."[6]

The Feminist Movement gave the same awakening to the field of literature too. Feminist criticism came into existence as part of Women's Liberation Movement and pointed out the anamorphic state and the distorted image of women in literature. Virginia Woolf's seminal book, *A Room of One's Own* published in 1927 geared up the movement against sexist paradigms. The author emphasized the importance of space and independence of individuals.

Simone de Beauvoir's much talked-about and quoted book, *The Second Sex* published in France in the year 1949 stormed the minds of many men and women and marked the beginning of a new era in the history of Feminist Movement. Her thought-provoking remarks and statements made people think and ponder; whether they liked them or not. In this regard what she told an interviewer is worth-quoting, "Onc day I wanted to explain myself to myself . . . the first thing I had to say was 'I am a woman.'"[7] There were mixed responses from the people, albeit those of anger and verbal attack against the author far outnumbered those of appreciation and appraisal at that time. However, the book could not be ignored and gradually it created a larger impact on its readers for it was the first great work by a woman unravelling the many-layered subjugation of women as no other work before had done to this length. The book attacked the age-old myths, literature, culture, religion, history, traditional values, etc. as they constitute male construct to accelerate male domination and women subjugation. It also deals with many fundamental questions like:

> How can a human being in woman's situation attain fulfillment? What roads are open to her? Which are blocked? How can independence be recovered in a state of dependency? What circumstances limit woman's liberty and how can they be overcome? These are the fundamental questions on which I would fain throw some light.[8]

With lots of research work and analysis from various angles, the book was able to provide a fresh perspective on almost every aspect of women's life.

Though all these books had a great influence in shaping the formation of ideas and concepts that led to the making of the movements, the book that actually sparked off the modern Feminist Movement was Betty Friedan's *The Feminine Mystique* published in the year 1963. After conducting interviews with various women who were apparently happy in their married life, she concluded that these women were just playing the socially expected role of wife and mother, thereby challenging the notion that women sought and found happiness and fulfillment in marriage and motherhood. She observed:

> For a woman, as for a man, the need for self-fulfillment, autonomy, self-realisation independence, individuality, self-actualization is as important as the sexual need, with as serious consequences when it's thwarted.[9]

Another important book with feminist slant was *Sexual Politics* published in the year 1969 by Kate Millett. Alison Light says:

> *Sexual Politics* attempts a far-reaching analysis of patriarchy, traced across cultures and history as the primary political institutions, the expression of the distribution of political power according to an original sexual division of labour. Patriarchy is thus envisaged as the hierarchical institutionalisation of the unequal roles and status given to the two biological genders 'the birthright priority whereby male rules females.'[10]

In this book, the author exposed the oppressive system of patriarchy that subjugated women from time immemorial by attacking the myth of Pandora, the presentation of women in the writings of D.H. Lawrence, Henry Miller, Norman Mailer and Jean Genet. She also criticized Freud and his psychoanalytical theory. She charged these male writers with bringing sexual politics to literature and misleading the readers with false and distorted images of women.

All these books greatly influenced the existing literature, and literary criticism and literary theory were no longer the male's domain. These literary feminists challenged the assumption that writers, readers and critics were all men. The exclusion of women as a group from the literary scene was protested and the Feminist Liberation Movement awakened their thinking. As observed by Elaine Showalter:

> It was through the women's liberation movement that we began to draw connection between our own work and our own lives, to note the disparities between identifications and ambitions that had attracted us, along with thousands of other women, to the study and teaching of literature, and limited and secondary roles granted to fictional heroines, women writers, or female scholars.
>
> Feminism spoke to our lived and literary experience with the fierce urgency of a revelation or a Great Awakening.[11]

The feminist movement became revolutionary and militant in nature with the rise of a large number of women who denounced all forms of restrictions and constraints so much so that they even opposed social institutions like marriage. They felt that marriage was the root cause of all forms of subjugation without which women's amelioration would be possible. Militant feminists, like Germaine Greer, wanted to abolish marriage as an institution. There was protest against almost every aspect of male domination. No doubt, the protest movement startled, shockingly surprised and puzzled people with traditional views. Even the press and other mass media made a mockery of these 'women's libbers':

> They were portrayed variously as rejecting both marriage and motherhood, they were unhappily married or divorced or single. Physi-

> cally unattractive, they were compensating for their 'failure' as women. Strident, hostile, hysterical, and maladjusted, they lacked human compassion and perspective.[12]

This sudden outburst of anger and rebellious nature of the feminists might not be appreciated but it was a necessary passing phase to expose and oppose the dominant culture. In fact, the very expression of anger and rebellion is a form of denouncing the dictates of the patriarchal system. Such aberrant behaviour of these women was the result of long suppression and oppression and the direct manifestation of their frustration and alienation in a culture where there were inequalities and injustices in every way of their life. However, some of them began to realize the limitation of their approach and felt the need to accept social institutions like marriage and the importance of motherhood. Nevertheless, they still emphasized the reformation of women's condition. They acknowledged the biological differences between men and women. Unlike those strident feminists, they were more considerate and objective in their approach and outlook, keeping in mind the necessary social roles of both the sexes. Though they were convinced by the distinct characteristics of men and women, they opposed all kinds of inequalities and injustices that unjustly meted out to women just because of their sex. They wanted every possible opportunity that men had been enjoying so far without any grudge, to develop their potential. As a member of the NOW's (National Organization for Women) board of directors, what Carden had stated deserves some attention:

> I want to have part in creating a new society. . . . I want women to have something to say in their own lives. . . . I have never reached my potential because of social conditions. I'm not going to get the rewards. I've been crippled. . . . I want to see the kind of systems that facilitates the use of potential.[13]

The new feminists' strategy, especially that of the French feminists, is based on the logic of sameness and difference between the two sexes. They do not feel ashamed of being women nor do they feel inferior to men. They seek to find out women's vision against all those men's vision that had already been before them since ages. What Viviane Forrester has observed in this regard is being cited:

> So what do men's eyes see? A crippled world, mutilated, deprived of women's vision. In fact men share our malaise, suffer from the same tragedy: the absence of women particularly in the field of cinema.
>
> If we were responsible for this absence, couldn't they complain about it? . . .
>
> We don't hear such complaints and for obvious reasons. Because this blindness to women's vision of the human species, has been fashioned by men for our mutual impoverishment.
>
> . . . Women's vision is what is lacking and this lack not only creates a vacuum but it perverts, alters, annuls every statement.[14]

They are positive in their approach and objective enough to see that men and women are 'different' and there is no question of superiority and inferiority. At the same time, they do not believe in the culturally constructed role of women and the strict role division of men and women both in domestic and in public spheres. They stiffly challenge the impositions and constraints on women and the relegation to make them 'the weaker sex.' This new breed of women begins to look at all the conventions and the aforesaid things critically. They even discard some feminist ideology which they think as 'male-identified' like that of Simone de Beauvoir. Their views are relationalistic rather than individualistic. They strive for the welfare of the society, ensuring that women should be provided with equal rights and equal opportunities with men. They visualize a well-balanced and harmonious relationship of men and women, instead of a discriminated one where men and women are constantly pouring hatred at each other.

The arrival of feminism in the field of literature has unravelled lots of misconceptions and misinterpretations of the image of women presented in various myths, folklore and other genres of literature. The feminist writers point out that myths are the creation of men to be used as an effective means to propagate women relegations and men supremacy. In myths and literature, women were often misrepresented and their images were distorted by either reducing their sizes or doubling them. Sometimes, women were put up on the pedestal and worshipped like goddesses, and sometimes, they were put down and treated like slaves, virtueless, vamps etc. In both the cases, they were being manipulated and used to serve the purpose of men as rightly stated by Jaidev, emphasizing the need to review such views and notions:

> We might also explain that too many of our fairy tales, folk tales and myths are anti-feminist, and that they are anti-feminist even when they worship women as deities and these therefore need to be rewritten or reinterpreted.[15]

The images of women even in holy books of various religions such as Christianity, Hinduism and Islam, to name a few, are not in favour of women. Feminists like Simone de Beauvoir, Betty Friedan and Kate Millett did not fail to see the conspicuous sexual politics presented in religious books like *The Bible* where Eve was projected as the cause of the downfall of human race. Since then, women have been blamed for and associated with sex and sin. The notion that Eve was created out of the supernumerary bone of Adam was decoded by these new feminists as some patriarchal designs used to forever push women to the margin behind men. In Hinduism, subjugation of women is operated at a complex level by using double mechanism—positive and negative. In positive mechanism, they praise women, treat them as goddesses, place them at the pedestal, epitomize them as the mother of all virtues, idealize and idolize them as Sita, Sati Savitiri, Damayanti etc., only to set golden rules for them to follow. The negative mechanism was so designed as reversed psychology by providing ugly alternatives in case they fail to follow the former mechanism. Here, women were projected as vamps who tried to disturb and destroy men in his attempt for higher pursuit. For example, the beautiful Menaka was made to disturb the Rishi Vishwamitra in his meditation, using her charm. In the *Ramayana* too, Supranakha was greatly humiliated and called seductress. In the *Mahabharata,* Amba was presented as 'unwomanly' for expressing anger and articulating her desire. In the holy book of Muslims, the *Quran*, a woman is described as 'fitna,' one who tempts man and brings trouble. All these points prove that even religion is not an exception while relegating women to the lower status.

These feminists are also equally aware of the sexual politics in literature and myths. They sense danger when women are being praised and idealized as much as when they are being criticized and looked down upon. By creating angelic and flawless women characters and making them the epitome of virtues, the male writers consciously or unconsciously contribute to further distortion of the image of woman. It is here, the new feminists feel the danger of internalization of these distorted images on the minds of women. It is a kind of setting ideal examples for all women to follow. The internalization of these concepts or misconcepts further propagates the same. In this way men can exploit women more by praising them. It is analogous to what Toni Morrison in her novel, *Beloved,* expresses that the Whites exploit the Blacks more through kindness and gentleness.

The new feminists also analyse and criticize the various writings of great writers, philosophers, psychologists and biologists and point out the grievances and destructions done by their works and how their writings and ideas directly or indirectly contribute to the deformation of the image of women as a group. For instance, the Greeks described women as 'womb,' thereby reducing women as only 'sexual objects' and 'child-bearing machines.' Even a great philosopher and scientist like Aristotle stated that women suffered from lack of certain qualities. St. Thomas described woman as 'imperfect man' and her being was 'incidental.' Likewise, scientists also contributed much to the terrible misconception of women with their fallacious findings and conclusions. For instance, in the 19th century, doctors were prevented from careful study of female reproductive system, believing certain biological factors made women temporarily insane and lifelong invalids. The anthropologists claimed that they found a particular kinship between women and animals and wrongly confirmed the notion that women were 'inferior beings' as compared to men. These notions were widespread and universal in the Western representation of women. Whether women were treated as angels or whores, in whatever position they were, women were always masked, branded as lower breeds. Aristotle, Descartes, Shakespeare, Dante, Pope and Fielding treated women with negative masks and attributes. Even Hardy, Joyce and Lawrence are blamed by feminists for overlooking the true image of women. This kind of treatment of women is based on the social and cultural construct, the prescribed model of woman as assumed by the patriarchal culture. Hence the treatment of women is stereotyped in male-produced texts.

The so-called 'scientific findings' as regards women, mentioned above, are not scientific, hence they had been disproved later. They played a great role in relegating women to the position of sub-human species in those days. These fallacious findings accelerated the view that women were not fit to hold responsibility, and that they needed to be guided and protected constantly. It was also believed that women lacked sexual feelings and were not able to attain orgasm. It was also wrongly concluded that those women who even attained it were 'viriloid' i.e. having the masculine characteristics. Such fallacious scientific findings greatly helped in the false representation of women, not knowing the true nature of women. Freudian analysis of women as deprived of orgasm and victim of 'penis envy' is biased male vision of women. A proper answer to such assumptions is given by French psychoanalytic feminists, like Kristeva.

One of the most path-breaking and epoch-making events in the history of literature is the arrival of feminist criticism that provides a totally new way of reading the texts that exist already. This new literary criticism deals with fundamental aspects about reading, writing and teaching of literature. As Sushila Singh observes: "Feminism has transformed the perceptions of life and literature. Literary theorists believe that feminist theory/criticism does not denote simply the addition of a new subject matter to an existing system of knowledge. By adding 'women' to literature, feminist criticism helps to expose the incompleteness of what once seemed universal."[16]

Another very important finding of feminist criticism is the massive recovery of women writers who had been obscured by male writers. Feminist writing and feminist criticism are subversive in order to challenge the male discourse on women. Feminist critics play a very important role in exposing such discrimination and partial treatment of women. They begin to re-read and reinterpret the existing male literature from feminist perspective and thereby, pointing out the incomplete and lopsided presentation of human experiences as presented in literature. This feminist reading of male-produced texts is called 'feminist critique,' a term invented by Showalter. They also feel the need to denounce the patriarchal literary canon and to reconstruct female literary tradition producing woman writing, called 'gynocritics' (Showalter) which is concerned "with woman as the producer of textual meaning, with the history, themes, genres and structures of literature by women. Its subjects include the psychodynamics of female creativity, linguistic and the problem of a female language; the trajectory of the individual or collective female literary career; literary history; and, of course, studies of particular writers and works."[17]

These avant-garde critics try to see some patterns and paradigms peculiar to the writings of women. One of the pioneers in this field, Elaine Showalter observes: "Many other critics are beginning to agree that when we look at women writers collectively we can see an imaginative continuum, the recurrence of certain patterns, themes, problems and images from generation to generation."[18]

These feminist critics unravel much confusion about feminism and literature. They clarify many hitherto vague terms like 'feminist' 'female' and 'feminine.'[19] Toril Moi defines 'feminist' as a political position, 'femaleness' as a matter of biology and 'femininity' as culturally construct characteristics of women. Kate Millett, in her book, *Sexual Politics*, expresses the need to expose the various ways and means of male dominance over female. The misinterpretation of women, their abuse and harassment in literary texts are under close scrutiny. These feminist critics are essentially polemical and also very radical in the sense that they are not only pluralistic in their approach towards literary methods and theories but also inventors of a new language and metaphor representing feminine consciousness, mind and body. Their aim is to have creative transformation.

Feminist criticism clears the doubts and solves the dilemma of many women writers who had been puzzled about whether they should write like their male counterparts by following the long masculine tradition or they should write the way they might choose—that is what they felt and thought. In this regard, the earlier phase of women writing such as the phase of Jane Austen, George Eliot may be stated. They, as women writers, did not make the complete break but simply wrote within the male writing tradition—just trying to get a female space in the mainstream male literature. But the whole perspective got changed when the twentieth century women started writing as for example, Virginia Woolf, Dorothy Richardson to name only a few. However, with the advent of the new literary theories, women have been freed of such doubts and have begun to express their bottled-up thoughts and emotions in their own language. Since then, there is a revolutionary change in the outlook and the way a literary work has been consumed. Many literary works that had been considered 'classic' and 'great' till then, have been censored and scrutinized. Lawrence Lipking says, "Something peculiar has been happening lately to the classics, some of them now seem less heroic, and some of them less funny."[20] The feminist critics also point out that not all literary works by women are necessarily feminist if their writings reflect the same stereotyped images of women as in most writings of men. As Rosalind Coward says:

> It is just not possible to say that woman-centred writings have any necessary relationship of feminism. The Mills and Boon romantic novels are written by, read by, marketed for, and are all about women. Yet nothing could be further from the aims of feminism than these fantasies based on sexual, racial and class submission which so frequently characterize these novels.[21]

In short, feminist writing is essentially 'political,' highly subversive and is able to deconstruct the patriarchal binary scheme and centre-margin dichotomy. Thus Feminism aims on the other hand at transforming the existing society on the basis of equality between the sexes and removal of the genderized principles with a view to bringing about a well-balanced social system, and on the other hand it tends to construct an alternative female tradition of writing.

Women's writing, which had started its history of writing from the time of Jane Austen, got momentum when women in the twentieth century wrote with conviction and commitment. They produced the history of women's painful experiences. The long confined life gave them a voice that was never heard in the past; it is full of poetic sensibility recreating silence in a language that is able to disturb communication through its vibrant fluid rhythm. Feminism is power politics that challenges the fixed centre while installing the marginal voice in the centre. This can be achieved by both the socially-oriented Anglo-American feminists who derived their strength from the fight for equal opportunities, equal treatment and equal rights, and the French psychoanalytical feminists who exploited language as a source of expression of their self as against the male power represented by the stable and fixed language system. Thus the symbolic order is deconstructed by the voice from the margin.

Feminism, thus, has many facets, and representing women's social, political, sexual and literary issues varies from culture to culture, race to race. Indian feminism is different from the Western feminism in which the conscious and educated women's problems are far different from the Indian one that faces problems peculiar to the culture and social realities of the country. Similarly, African and Arab feminisms have their own distinctive problems and issues. Now, attention may be drawn to Indian feminism. The Western feminism could not penetrate Indian soil as swiftly and easily as it had done in other European countries. Nevertheless, it came slowly but surely, and consolidated its position amidst various unfavourable circumstances.

India is a country, which has its rich and long historical, social, cultural and religious background. It is the birthplace of many religions of which Hinduism is the main. It is a land where women deities are worshipped. Behind this seemingly respected status of women, what they face in real life is often quite the contrary. From morning till night, they're engaged in household chores, bearing and rearing children. They were/are not allowed to participate in family discussions, not to mention public affairs like politics and other social matters, the underlying meaning being that women are not fit and valid for such higher faculties which are often considered as men's domain. Even today, the image of Indian woman has remained the same—self-sacrificing, ever-forgiving, loving, caring and kind-hearted, guardians of virtues who bear everything with a smile without any complaint. Women have been trained from the very beginning to internalize these concepts. Though some change in the attitude of both men and women is discernible, it is, unfortunately, not reachable to most people in the country.

Education and feminism play a very important part in the present mindset of people. They find almost everything that had been considered normal, questionable. These groups of people begin to see the need to review many religious books and scriptures, like the *Upanishads*, the great epics, the *Vedas*, the great classics from a new perspective. It is so conspicuous that these scriptures were written by men to fashion and design a certain paradigm that would propagate their supremacy over women for all the time to come. No wonder, women were not allowed to read and study these scriptures for a long time. For example, in the *Rig Veda*, it is said that women are bereft of intelligence and hence, not fit for education and higher faculties. Such terrible misconception about women enhances women subjugation. In recent decades, women outscore men at various levels—school, college and university. The reason why women could not do so from the very beginning is that they had been denied the opportunities (to prove themselves) that men had been enjoying from time immemorial.

Of all the scriptures, *Manu Smriti* has greatly influenced and affected the life of women. Manu, the ancient law-giver of Hindu society laid myriad roles and duties for women from childhood to death:

> *Manu Smriti* (200 B.C.) prescribes duties and obligations for a woman from childhood to death. According to it, she should be a perpetual minor, to be under the guardianship of some one or the other. . . . Even if the husband is immoral, a debauch, and lacks good qualities the wife must still worship him as if he were god himself. (Manu 5-154). . . . A woman need not perform any yagna or ceremony or undertake any fast for her salvation. She will attain better life by service to her husband only. [22]

All these preaching have served men's interest at the expense of women for a long time. Such discrimination and partial treatment of women have resulted in wide disparity between masculine and feminine world.

Repeated indoctrination of such notions and beliefs inflicted on women severely debilitates them. The practice of 'sati,' child-marriage, celibacy of widowhood, female infanticide, dowry system etc., paralyzed the spirit of Hindu women. Even today, some of the social evils are practised despite various laws enforced against them. The condition of Muslim women is worst. The 'purdah' system is still observed by many. The conditions of women in Muslim communities, in and outside the country, are still deplorable. 'Honour Killing,' 'Honour Suicide' are very much prevalent and practised despite various laws against them. It is ironical that the community that allows men to get married four times, forces women to kill themselves (Honour Suicide) or to be killed by their kins in the name of saving family's honour for slight and minor aberration on their parts. An article in *Times of India* describing one such incident is cited when Muslim women were "stoned to death, strangled, shot or buried alive. Their offences ranged from stealing a glance at a boy to wearing a short skirt, wanting to go to the movies, being raped by a stranger or relative or having consensual sex. . . . The organization (U.N.O.) estimates that 5,000 women are killed each year around the world by relatives who accuse them of bringing dishonour on their families."[23]

Both men and women have been so brainwashed and conditioned to ward off age-old tradition, concepts and culture. Women have been subjected to such inhuman treatment all through in the name of honour, religion, tradition and culture while men have been enjoying every possible advantage. In many incidents, society looks down upon the rape victims and sometimes they are even punished but not the rapists. Such ugly realities and injustices rule over many lives behind the façade of modernity. These are the evils which feminism vehemently strives to completely wipe out to bring about a new world where the binary opposition of men and women meet at a point for mutual benefit and common welfare.

Pioneers of Indian writing in English—Mulk Raj Anand, R.K. Narayan and Raja Rao and many other writers fail to present women realistically in their fiction. Most women characters are presented as victims of social injustice. These male writers create too idealistic and virtuous women that are hard to believe like Kajoli in *So Many Hungers!* by Bhabani Bhattacharya. Though these novelists fail to create role model women characters, they do present individuals who have the need to attain personal fulfillment in their careers like Rosie in R.K. Narayan's *The Guide*.

Talking about writing about women by men and women writers, Y.S. Sunita Reddy opines, "men tend to go to extremes either highlighting their weaknesses or deifying them and putting them on the pedestal, making the characters seem unreal. Women writers, on the other hand are more honest in their portrayal of women in their novels."[24]

Women novelists like Kamala Markandaya, Anita Desai, Nayantara Sahgal, Shashi Deshpande, Arundhati Roy and Shobha De portray women characters, their inner psyche, hopes and fears, insecurities and frustrations, feelings and sentiments, etc. more realistically than their male counterparts. In their writings, women's untold stories have been told; women's lives and their problems are dealt with authentically. For instance, Anita Desai's forte as a novelist lies in her portrayal of the disturbed psyche of hypersensitive modern women and their predicaments. Most of her women characters tend to take extreme steps when they are no longer able to bear the intensity of their sufferings in an alien and hostile circumstance. They tend to take violent steps like Maya in *Cry, the Peacock* (1980), Nanda Kaul in *Fire on the Mountain* (1999) who commit suicide. Though these women novelists make successful attempts to portray women honestly and realistically, they fail to provide a satisfying solution in most cases. However, their writings are one way of showing defiance against the male tradition/ power/ hegemony. As Madhumalati Adhikari says: "The women hero's triumph or defeat, despite a valiant struggle is a mode of defying patriarchy. A woman's story inevitably silenced by the androcentric culture, narrated from a woman's point of view by women itself is a defiance of male power."[25]

Shashi Deshpande, a prolific writer, makes a wise choice by selecting middle class women as her protagonists. Of all the classes, middle class tends to regard the social, moral, cultural and religious codes and disciplines more seriously than any other class. The middle class mindset gives much importance to ethics, and truthfully follows the socially accepted paradigm. Of late, this class receives, perhaps, the greatest blow of the avant-garde modern feminism in India. They are in a fix, and mentally disturbed when they find lots of contradiction between the age-old beliefs and customs and the new ideas they get from education and feminism. They are torn apart between traditional beliefs and modern outlook. Shashi Deshpande, as a novelist, exposes the problems and predicaments, dilemmas, hopes and aspirations, failures and insecurities of these women under such circumstances. It is interesting to note how finally, the protagonists come to terms with their divided selves, and start life afresh with hopes of better tomorrows as they are able to gain self-realization.

NOTES

1. Alice Jardine, *Gynesis: Configurations of Women and Modernity* (Ithaca: Cornell University Press, 1986), 20.
2. Herbert Marder, *Feminism and Art: A Study of Virginia Woolf* (Chicago and London: The University of Chicago Press, 1968), 2.
3. Guerin at al., *A Handbook of Critical Approaches to Literature* (New York: OUP, 1999), 196.
4. Kelly Joan, *Women, History, Theory: The Essays of Joan Kelly* (Chicago: University of Chicago Press, 1984), 69.
5. Sushila Singh, "Feminism: The Movement and the Ideology" *Feminism: Theory, Criticism, Analysis* (New Delhi: Pencraft International, 1997), 15.
6. John Stuart Mill, *The Subjection of Women* (Rpt. Cambridge: The I.T. Press, 1989), 3.
7. Qtd. Deirdre Bair, "Introduction to the Vintage Edition," *The Second Sex,* trans. and ed. H.M. Parshley (Rpt. New York: Vintage, 1989), viii.
8. Simone de Beauvoir, "Introduction" *The Second Sex*, xxxv.

9. Friedan Betty, *The Feminine Mystique* (Rpt. Harmondsworth: Penguin, 1971), 282.
10. Alison Light, "Feminism and the Literary Critic," Mary Eagleton, ed., *Feminist Literary Theory: A Reader* (Rpt. Massachusetts: Blackwell, 1996), 242.
11. Elaine Showalter, ed. *The New Feminist Criticism: Essays on Women, Literature and Theory* (New York: Pantheon, 1985), 5.
12. Maren Lockwood Carden, *The New Feminist Movement* (New York: Russell Sage Foundation, 1974), xviii.
13. *Ibid.*, 12.
14. Viviane Forrester, "'What Women's Eyes See: New French Feminists," Mary Eagleton, ed., *Feminist Literary Theory*, 57.
15. Jaidev, "Problematizing Feminism," Sushila Singh, ed., *Feminism and Recent Fiction in English* (New Delhi: Prestige, 1991), 62.
16. Sushila Singh, "Preface" *Feminism: Theory, Criticism, Analysis*, 8.
17. Elaine Showalter, "Towards a Feminist Poetics," Philip Rice and Patricia Waugh, ed., *Modern Literary Theory: A Reader* (Rpt. London: Edward Arnold, 1992), 92-93.
18. Elaine Showalter, "Literature of Their Own: British Women Novelists from Bronte to Lessing," Mary Eagleton, ed., *Feminist Literary Theory,* 14.
19. Toril Moi, "Feminist Literary Criticism," Ann Jefferson and David Robey, ed., *Modern Literary Theory* (London: B.T. Batsford, 1986), 204.
20. Lawrence Lipking, "Aristotle's Sister: A Poetics of Abandonment," *Critical Inquiry*, 10 September (1983): 79.
21. Rosalind Coward, "This Novel Changes Women's Lives: Are Women's Novels Feminist Novels," *Feminist Review*, 5 (1980): 230.
22. Qtd. Malladi Subbamma, *Women, Tradition and Culture*, trans. M. V. Ramamurty (New Delhi: Sterling, 1985), 16-17.
23. Dan Bilefsky, "Now, 'honour suicide' in Turkey," *Times of India* 17 July 2006, 16.
24. Y.S. Sunita Reddy, "Introduction" *A Feminist Perspective on the Novels of Shashi Deshpande* (New Delhi: Prestige, 2001), 17.
25. Madhumalati Adhikari, "Defying Patriarchy: Female Protagonists in Virginia Woolf's *Mrs. Dalloway*, Toni Morrison's *Beloved* and Anita Desai's *Clear Light of Day*," *Points of View*, Vol. II, No. 1, (Summer 1995), 85.

Deshpande's Concept of Feminism

> Today, when I call myself a feminist, I believe that the female of the species has the same right to be born and survive, to fulfill herself and shape her life according to her needs and the potential that lies within her as the male has. I believe that women are neither inferior nor subordinate human beings, but one half of the human race.[1]

Considering the above statement, Deshpande's concept of feminism is analogous to the modern feminism that emphasizes the need of self-realization and self-actualization of women as individuals. In the essay, "Why I am a feminist," Deshpande expresses her idea of feminism in a nutshell. She is not happy with the way people in India, specially those women who are in influential position give such misleading statements that they are not feminists because they do not hate men, the implication being that feminists are men haters. In India, people have terrible misconception about feminism that it is often regarded as "a Western concept, rejecting the family and home, hating men and waging a war against them."[2] She expresses her concern about this wrong notion and its possible impact on the minds of common readers who are not well-informed about the actual concept of feminism. In the same essay, the novelist opines that feminism is not about wanting to be like man but a graceful acceptance of womanhood as a positive thing, not lack of something. She considers a woman a different being from man but not inferior to him. She is much against self-sacrificing image of women in Indian society that denies their individuality. She believes in the institution of family that works for the benefit of all society. It should not be built on the sacrifice of some but on the co-operation and compromises of all its members for the common welfare.

The novelist seems to be against those militant feminists that discard the value of family, rush for a divorce even for a minor reason, etc. She further observes that there are some women who actually are happy being housewives and they should not be forced to have careers. Nevertheless, she expresses her concern over the need to support oneself. She is not against motherhood but condemns women being reduced to nothing but child-bearing and rearing machines. Deshpande shares her concept and aims of feminism with that of the modern feminism that strives for self-actualization. As Carden says:

> The New feminism is not about the elimination of differences between the sexes; nor even simply the achievement of equal opportunity: it concerns the individual's right to find out the kind of person he or she is and to strive to become that person.[3]

Shashi Deshpande, as a writer, authentically sketches her characters and truthfully reveals their inner psyche, their problems and predicaments, hopes and aspiration, frustrations and sufferings. Her treatment of women characters in her writings is to provide a fresh perspective to the image and roles of women in a patriarchal society like India. As a writer, she does not follow the much tried and tested masculine traditions and theories of writing; instead, she writes as a woman novelist about women installing a female tradition wherein lies the inner working of the minds of women. Her language, vision and expression are authentically female in the sense that they give expression to the female experience, real, mental, emotional and psychological, all able to integrate female life in various aspects. Her women protagonists are well-aware of the masculine framework and tradition-bound culture of our society. They are conscious of their 'secondary position' and victimization. Their self-realization is treated by the novelist as the first stepping-stone towards their emancipation as individuals. Her attempt to make honest portrayal of women and the realistic presentation of their problems, their anger and reactions against the male-domination, makes her novels worth studying. She is guarding herself against being called a feminist and her novels against being read as feminist texts.

Deshpande's feminism as reflected in her novels is not a hardcore militant type. Through her writings, her opposition against patriarchal domination and system is discernible; however, her opposition is never directed against individual men. Ranjini is right when she says of Shashi Deshpande: "Not being a militant feminist she does not attribute to man the sole cause of women's problems."[4] Deshpande, as a novelist, is relatively free from prejudices against men as we often find in most writings about women, and it makes her writings all the more convincing and authentic. Unlike those feminist writers who, while desperately trying to drive home certain points and trying to fit some feminist theories, end up creating wooden characters, she chooses to let loose the human emotion. As a writer, she seems to preoccupy herself with human relationships and emotions, besides her concern over women's predicaments, as she says in an interview:

> Human relationship is what a writer is involved with person to person and person to society relationships—these are the primary concerns of a creative writer and, to me, the former is of immense importance. My preoccupation is with interpersonal relationships and human emotions.[5]

At times, Shashi Deshpande seems to be more a humanist than a feminist. If feminist thought is "humanist" thought, then she is a feminist writer par excellence.

As already discussed in chapter II, Elaine Showalter divides the writings of women into three phases—"the feminine phase," "the feminist phase" and "the female phase"—to show the growth and development of women's writing. When we study the women characters in many of the novels of Shashi Deshpande, we find that they also have a similar kind of growth and development of their characters—not the writing history of women as stated by Showalter. Deshpande's protagonists as individuals seem to pass through all the three phases but in the order of ''feminist',' "feminine'' and "female" phases. Most of her protagonists are often critical about the existing gender imbalance and question the unequal treatment of men and women in the society. Some of them even defy the dictate of patriarchy and challenge the system openly by protesting and rejecting the social and cultural set-up like the marriage institution. There are so many instances in the novels where the protagonists assert their rights and privileges by rejecting the traditional norms much to the agitation and opposition from their respective families. As a result, some of them have to pay high price for their defiance. They look at things differently, and put forth their problems and reactions first as to pull down the traditional impositions on women. To voice, to question becomes the primary preoccupation of these new women, and instead of becoming weak and docile characters. They try to fulfill their individual rights and wishes. Meera Bai writes:

> Modern women find no sense in being an acquiescent, suffering and sacrificing lot. As they feel the need for self-expression and individual fulfillment, they have begun to question the conventions and defy traditions. This craving for individual freedom naturally results in breaking up of family and relationships.[6]

A few of Shashi Deshpande's novels bear witness to this. In the first place, we can take up *The Dark Holds No Terrors*. In this novel, Saru, the protagonist is well aware of the unequal treatment of her and her brother Dhruva by her parents and family subjecting a girl child to take secondary position even at her own home. She questions and complains about such treatment. For example, she takes exception to the celebrations of her birthdays which are never like those of her brother. As a child, she is much disturbed by the way her parents treat her brother differently, and ignoring her. She protests that she be given equal treatment by her parents. Such negligence of girl by her own parents has a long-lasting negative impact on the future life of the child. In Saru's case, such thoughts like "Nobody likes me. Nobody cares for me. Nobody wants me" (83) haunt her and the feeling of her being unwanted has remained a psychic residue in her character. This has affected the whole of her life, mentally, emotionally and psychologically. Deshpande seems to point out the danger of forcing such negative image of oneself on the girl child by subjecting them to unequal treatment at such an impressionable age.

Saru suffers from acute sense of inferiority complex. Outwardly, she appears to be a dominant sister to her brother, a hostile daughter to her mother but inwardly, she is a pathetic child who tries to attract the attention she hardly gets, that kind of utmost care and affection her brother has been showered upon. For an inquisitive child like her, such unhealthy atmosphere of her childhood deeply affects her all through her life. From then onwards, she reacts against all forms of domination and restrictions. She defies her mother openly and challenges the traditional norms. She develops a kind of hatred for her mother (who is, to her, a symbol of domination) to the extent that she thinks, "If you're a woman, I don't want to be one" (62). She studies hard to prove herself and to give a reason to live, a purpose of her life, and most importantly, to answer her mother's cruel question, "why didn't you die? Why are you alive, when he's dead?" (191), charging Saru that she had killed her brother.

Rebellion and defiance become her second nature. Saru deliberately ignores her mother's presence and questions when the latter asks about her decision to join medicine as a career. Saru talks to her father instead, pleading him to let her join medicine. The following conversation clearly shows Saru's indifferent attitude towards her mother:

> 'I want to do medicine,' I said. . . .
>
> 'You mean you want to become a doctor?'
>
> I did not reply. I would not answer her. I stared at Baba instead, waiting for him to say something.
>
> 'Baba,' I said, louder this time. 'I said I want to go in for medicine.'
>
> 'Where's the college?'
>
> Again I ignored her and spoke to him.
>
> 'Shall I send in my application, Baba?'
>
> We were like the three points of a triangle, eternally linked, forever separate. (141)

When her father finally agrees, much to the opposition of her mother, Saru's happiness is doubled. Later on, she marries Manohar, a man of her choice who is also a low caste, causing opposition from her parents. She asserts her individuality by defying the traditional mode of arranged marriage. She becomes a successful doctor and smart young lady who knows her worth and how to use influential people like Boozie, her teacher on medical staff, to further her career.

There is a drastic change in the personality of Saru even to her own surprise. After marriage, she becomes more and more successful and her husband, is still there, teaching in a third rate college. She becomes a victim of domestic violence at the hands of her husband. She is now two different persons—one who acts as a confident doctor during daytime, and another, a terrified being, during nights. She is subjected to sexual assault when her husband turns a sadist just to prove his masculinity. Saru is no longer independent in spirit, though she seems to be the same independent woman. "It was strange that after all these years of having been in full control of her life, she now had this great desire to let go" (97).

From being independent, fearless woman who rejected any kind of domination that came her way, she becomes fearful, terrified, afraid of the dark, engulfing nights. It seems her feminist phase—a time when she opposed and reacted against traditional impositions—is over, followed on close heels the feminine phase by force of circumstances. She lets herself loose to be carried away by social norms whether she likes it or not. She speaks of sexual politics of which women are always victims, of biologism, that makes a divide between man and woman, husband and wife much to the advantage of man. And a woman has to accept that secondary and oppressed position that does not give women to raise their position higher than their husbands' although they have better performance and ability to prove their worth. Such women fall victims to sexual harassment at home. Saru in a lecture on medicine as a career for women at a girls' college goes on to attack male hegemony in a rather ironical tone that hides and suggests her contempt for brute masculinity of man. Instead of talking on the topic concerned, Saru pours out her emotions and feelings arising out of her bitter experiences:

> A wife must always be a few feet behind her husband. If he's an M.A., you should be a B.A. If he's 5'4" tall, you shouldn't be more than 5'3" tall. If he's earning five hundred rupees, you should earn not more than four hundred and ninety-nine rupees. That's the only

> rule to follow if you want a happy marriage. Don't ever try to reverse the doctor-nurse, executive-secretary, principal-teacher role. It can be traumatic, disastrous. And, I assure you, it isn't worth it. He'll suffer, you'll suffer and so will the children. Women's magazines will tell you that a marriage should be an equal partnership. That's nonsense. Rubbish. No partnership can ever be equal. It will always be unequal, but take care that it's unequal in favour of your husband. If the scales tilt in your favour, god help you, both of you. (137)

Then comes the final phase—the female phase of self-discovery—at the very end of the novel. After her mother's death, Saru visits her parents' home and stays there, ostensibly to take care of her father, but actually to escape from her husband's nightmarish brutality. It is here that she begins to introspect and retrospect about her life, her past, and it serves as a healing process to her wounded 'psyche.' Like most of Shashi Deshpande's protagonists, Saru too is facing 'middle life crisis' when "instead of looking forward one looks backward . . . and begins to take stock, to see how one's life has developed up to this point."[7] She realizes that she has been blaming herself for all the past errors and mistakes and punishing herself by bearing and remaining stoically silent.

Even at the beginning of the last chapter, she is not sure of herself when she receives a telegram from her husband saying that he's coming to take her. She is afraid to face him and asks her father to promise not to open the door when he comes. In fact, when Saru musters up her courage and narrates the whole incidents to her father, of how she has been tortured by her husband during nights, it acts as a kind of 'Catharsis' and relieves her from self-inflicted diseases. Her father's kind and affectionate words soothe her. Slowly, she realizes, "If I have been a puppet it is because I made myself one. I have been clinging to the tenuous shadow of a marriage whose substance has long since disintegrated because I have been afraid of proving my mother right" (220). Here, through the character of Saru, Deshpande seems to convey a significant truth regarding the relegation of women that, in most cases, women are responsible for their lot and they have the power to control and improve their life if they are determined to do so. In this context, what Gandhiji had observed as regards the British colonization of India as analogous to patriarchal colonization of women is well-worth quoting: "The English have not taken India; we have given it to them. They are not in India because of their strength, but because we keep them."[8]

It is apparent that through this novel the novelist lays emphasis on the need and importance of having a profession or a career of woman of her own. It's not only because of the financial independence but also because of the emotional satisfaction one's profession helps in self-assertion. In the present novel, Saru's self-assertion regains when a neighbouring child comes to call her to see his ailing sister. Her role as a doctor overtakes and she is charged and confident with her professional proficiency. When everything about her seems to fail—her role as a daughter, sister, wife and mother—it is her role as a doctor that saves her and asserts her individuality. She realizes her worth and no longer is afraid of darkness. We see a different Saru when she says, "And, oh yes, Baba, if Manu comes, tell him to wait. I'll be back as soon as I can" (221), ready to face anyone and anything. She takes and holds the reins of her life, 'My life is my own' (220). She is sure of herself for 'the dark holds no terrors' for her. At the end, she is no longer the bitter woman who says 'no' to struggle but the one who is ready to struggle hard and swim against the tide, not to get drowned but remain floating always.

Saru, like most protagonists of Deshpande, passes through three phases. At the beginning, she is an angry young woman, questioning, protesting and defying any form of domination. After marriage, she becomes timid following the dictates of the society and the roles as prescribed by culture. Lastly, she can attain a kind of selfhood that leads her to a more secure, meaningful and independent life. As Sunita Reddy writes: "Deshpande's protagonists are, no doubt, victims of this unequal power structure in marriage, but in all her novels she shows how one can rise above such injustice and lead a meaningful existence."[9]

What has been pointed out by the novelist is the realization of her protagonists of their own blind spots besides those of others around them, and most importantly, they are ready to rectify them. In this sense, it may be said that Saru has completed the full circle of the feminist, the feminine and the female phases, recuperating her self-image in the last phase.

Indu, the protagonist of the next novel, *Roots and Shadows* is, perhaps, the most committed feminist among her protagonists. She is an extremely independent and intelligent woman who is 'child-less by choice' which is quite unthinkable and rare in Indian society where women are being looked down upon for being barren. Even such a fiercely independent woman like her, passes through all the three phases mentioned above, at some point or the other. Like Saru, she defies the traditional norms by getting married to the man of her choice who is from a different caste, much against the wishes and opposition from her family, especially from Akka, her father's aunt who warns her, "Such marriages never work. Different castes, different languages . . . it's all right for a while. Then they realise" (68).

Indu has a strong view against the traditional arranged marriage where everything is considered except the emotions and feelings of the bride to be. Indu cannot believe like those traditional women who religiously follow the tradition as she says:

> It disgusted me to see the strewn plates, the scattered remnants. And yet, for a whole lifetime, the women patiently cleared up the mess with their bare hands after each meal. And women like Kaki even ate off the same dirty plate their husbands had eaten in earlier. Martyrs, heroines, or just stupid fools? (67)

She discards the traditional belief by calling her husband by name. She cannot see any reasonable link between calling one's husband by name and the longevity of his life. When she is reminded of such things, she reacts sharply:

> 'They, they, they,' I exclaimed impatiently. 'Who are they? That's just to frighten the women. To keep them in their places. And poor fools, we do just that. What connection can there be between a man's longevity and his wife's calling him by name? It's as bad as praying to the tulsi to increase his life span.' (32)

Indu is not a blind follower of such rituals and dictated duties of women. No wonder, she defies Akka, who exercises her authority over the lives of other members of the family, laying out so many 'dos' and 'don'ts' to them.

It is hard to believe that such an independent woman will one-day succumb to the social conditioning, and internalize the accepted norms, which she has vehemently opposed and rejected. When she was told that as a girl, she should be "obedient and unquestioning," "meek and submissive" she questioned "why?" When she had seen all the women follow the norms, she had laughed at them, and sworn, "I would never pretend to be what I was not" (185). Ironically, this is exactly what she does, pretending what she is not. Slowly and steadily, the process of metamorphosis from being feminist to feminine works out bit by bit, sometimes consciously and at others unconsciously. She has loosened the reins of her own life, letting her husband hold them, according to the tradition. When she comes to know that "it shocks him to find passion in a woman" (83), she learns her lesson (like all those women she had once laughed at) to pretend and remain passive and unresponsive. She realizes what her marriage has taught her, "to reveal to Jayant nothing but what he wanted to see, to say to him nothing but what he wanted to hear" and "to hide responses and emotions as if they were bits of garbage" (38). Now, she becomes almost like those women whom she did not like to become. Perhaps, the only difference is that these women may do blindly or uncritically but she, critically.

Coming and staying at her parents' home after long years to see the dying Akka, Indu gets an opportunity to introspect her past life from a distance. She realizes how independently she grew up and how marriage and tradition influence her as a person as she confides to her cousin and childhood friend Naren, of how the contours of her life have drastically changed as per the pattern drawn by the society. She is objective to see her own faults and does not fall to the categories of women who always blame others and society except themselves as she says, "And I can't blame him. It is not he who has pressurized me into this. It's the way I want it to be" (49).

Indu now awakens her inner self and begins to search her identity: "Am I on my way to becoming an ideal woman? A woman who sheds her 'I' who loses her identity in her husband's?" (29). She realizes she had been playing the stereotyped roles in both her personal life, as a wife and her professional life, as a writer, by writing "through the eyes of a man" (79). As a writer, she has rejected her womanhood and individual self, following the long line of masculine culture. She is a failure in her personal and professional life. She begins to see that she "had clung tenaciously to Jayant, to her marriage, not for love alone," but because she "was afraid of failure." She had to show that her marriage "was a success to the world" (159).

This self-examination leads to self-realization, which ultimately leads to self-assertion. Towards the end of the novel, a different Indu emerges as she asserts herself as a person and no longer denies the fact that she is a woman. She does not harbour any guilt feelings over her physical encounter with Naren. She determines not to tell about it to her husband as she feels that it has nothing to do with their life together. Now, Indu becomes a whole person again, having and exercising her rights. Her independent decision over how to use the money and property Akka had given to her before her death is a proof of her self-assertion:

> That I was resigning from my job. That I would at last do the kind of writing I had always dreamt of doing. That I would not, could not enrich myself with Akka's money. That I would, on the other hand, pay for Mini's wedding.
>
> Maybe Jayant would understand. Maybe he wouldn't. But even so. (187)

Indu, finally, after much struggle over her mental journey, attains self-realization, which according to Elaine Showalter is the phase of femaleness. In this regard, what S.P. Swain has said is worth-mentioning:

> Thus Indu's uncompromising and paradoxical feminine self that frantically longed for self-expression, finally finds its roots in the home and with her husband. Shadows disappear from her vision and she sees the clear light of day with the realization and discovery of her authentic female self.[10]

The protagonist of Deshpande's novel *That Long Silence,* that won the Sahitya Akademi Award in 1991, is married for seventeen years to Mohan and has got two children. It is at the Dadar flat where they have come and stayed for a while, (to avoid scandal as Mohan had been accused of business malpractice) that Jaya begins to look at her life, now and then, and tries to bridge the huge differences between her past—before marriage—and her post-marriage life to lead a more meaningful and harmonious life. Jaya grows up as an independent young girl who questions the differences, the inequalities that exist in the society so much so that her "ajji" remarks, "I feel sorry for your husband Jaya, whoever he is. Look at you—for everything a question, for everything a retort. What husband can be comfortable with that?" (27) She is quite different from these women who believe that "a husband is like a sheltering tree" (32). She ignores them and their ideas and beliefs. She is also critical of all the fasting and endless pujas performed by her aunts. She sees the futility and meaninglessness of performing such rituals to serve any particular purpose. She is quite unorthodox and radical in her views and approaches before marriage.

After marriage, Jaya becomes "Suhasini," the name given by her husband. With this new name, Jaya is introduced to a new model where femininity is being celebrated. She learns not to question, not to retort as she says, "I had neither any questions nor any retorts for Mohan now" (27). She had learnt to be silent and she is even ready to bandage like Gandhari to everything her husband does. Like mythical woman, Sita, she blindly follows her husband wherever he goes and does whatever he tells her. Marriage has made her a totally different person. It takes her name, her identity and her independence as Simone de Beauvoir states:

> Marriage has always been a very different thing for man and for woman. The two sexes are necessary to each other, but this necessity has never brought about a condition of reciprocity between them; women as we have seen, have never constituted a caste making exchanges and contracts with the male caste upon a footing of equality.[11]

Marriage and social set-up contribute to the relegation of women, and deter them from asserting their individuality. Her husband becomes her "profession," her "career" and her "means of livelihood" (75). Everything she does revolves round her husband, even her haircut and dresses. When her mother asks, "Have you gone mad? All your lovely hair!" she replies calmly, "Mohan wanted to cut it" (96). This Jaya is quite different from the Jaya who had been quite independent and had resisted her mother's slight probing of her whereabouts, "She can't dictate to me! I'll do just what I want!" (75) Now, she becomes a stereotyped woman who is "scared of cockroach, lizards, nervous about electrical gadgets, hopeless at technical matter, lazy about accounting . . . almost the stereotype of a woman: nervous incompetent needing male help and support" (76).

Now Jaya has to stop promoting all her past concepts of how women should live (in the feminist sense) and has to relearn how to live safely without any complaints in a male-dominated society accepting those traditional values and norms. She realizes that as a married woman she has to hype up the image of her husband in the same fashion Virginia Woolf has remarked of the role of women as looking glasses to magnify the figure of man double its normal size. She also learns that anger makes a woman "unwomanly," and hence women are not supposed to express anger. In her early days of marriage, she asks Mohan to "do the cooking" (81) at which her husband takes it as merely a joke. She becomes aware of the strict role-division among men and women. She comes to realize that women have no place that they can call their own. They neither belong to their parents' family nor to their husbands.'

After a long silence, Jaya finally comes to the phase of self-realization or the female phase. She stops blaming others for her failures. She examines her past life and comes to know the truth about her failure as a writer. She had stopped writing good stuff because of her own fear of failure. Looking through her diaries, she realizes that all these years she had been "Mohan's wife. Rahul's and Rati's mother" (69) but not herself. She had been denying herself completely. She cannot relate or connect to the kind of person she had been. At present, she is no longer a fragmented self and no longer afraid of anything:

> I'm not afraid any more. The panic has gone. I'm Mohan's wife, I had thought, and cut off the bits of me that had refused to be Mohan's wife. Now, I know that kind of fragmentation is not possible. (191)

"Self-revelation is a cruel process" (1) but it is through this process that self-realization comes. This self-realization is so important as it leads one to a positive direction. Jaya, at the end of the novel, is aware of "so many crossroads, so many choices" (192) that life has offered. She finally makes up her mind to break "that long silence" she had been nurturing as she says, "I will have to speak, to listen, I will have to erase the silence between us"—between her and her husband (192). In this connection, what Shirin Kudchedkar has opined holds true of women protagonists of Shashi Deshpande:

> Women come to realize the inauthenticity of the lives led and struggle to discover for themselves their own impulses, reactions, desires and needs. Their quest is for self-knowledge and self-realization which can in turn lead to relationships based on mutual understanding and respect.[12]

The remaining novels—*A Matter of Time*, *The Binding Vine*, *Small Remedies, Moving On* and the latest, *In the Country of Deceit*—are somewhat different in theme and structure, and hence the need of a different reading of the protagonists of these novels is called for. These protagonists are comparatively older, wiser and mature enough to deal with life's uncertainties, except Devayani or Devi. They stoically undergo their problems and predicaments in their own ways, and try to bring harmony amidst the chaos. It is worth-noting that the novelist makes a successful attempt to treat her women characters as individuals, who grow and develop not in the same pattern of feminist, feminine and femaleness like their earlier counterparts. But each one is able to cope with all these conflicting selves of woman so as to make each woman a well-rounded character with these complex ideas merged into one personality.

In *A Matter of Time*, Sumi, the protagonist, accepts the greatest tragedy of her life with stoic silence when her husband, Gopal walks out of their marriage and family. She, along with her three teenage daughters, has to come back to stay with her parents. Being an independent woman who does not have to depend on others, she tries every means to search for a rented house and tries to be financially independent. She never entertains the idea of being a parasite on others, even on her own parents.

In this novel, Aru, the eldest daughter of Sumi, represents the feminist phase of protest. She almost becomes a hard-core militant feminist when she finds everything around her in a big chaos. She wonders how her mother can hold herself and remain unaffected by all these terrible happenings in their life after her father had left them. She demands justice and even goes to contact a lady lawyer to sue her father as she feels that "he can't get away scot-free. He shouldn't be able to do this and just walk away" (137-38). She has begun to see a victim in every woman, a betrayer in every man, much to the disturbance of her mother. Seeing her grandparents' and parents' unsuccessful married life, Aru, at the age of eighteen, becomes so bitter of life that she resolves, 'I'm never going to get married" (76). She confides to her aunt, "I've been thinking about marriage a great deal, Premi-mashi. What is there in it? I mean, look at Amma and now Sumi. . . . What do you get out of it?" (138)

Sumi is worried for her; she wants her daughter "to taste life," "to relish it and not spit it out because she finds it bitter" (220). Being more mature, Sumi can look at life and human beings with an understanding and an objective view. After Sumi's sudden and unexpected death along with her father in an accident, it is Aru who consoles and comforts everyone. There is no longer any hatred towards her father. Instead she encourages him to go, "Yes, Papa, you go. We'll be all right, we'll be quite all right, don't worry about us" (246). There is "undoubtedly, tolerance, love, kindness and faithfulness" which "are widely acknowledged traits of female nature" in her but Aru's "self-assertion is not to be viewed as contrary to these values. It is on this point that the feminist in Shashi Deshpande steps in."[13] Aru's self-realization and awareness of her female self is perceptible at the end of the novel.

In *The Binding Vine* too, the novel revolves round three stories—of Urmila, the protagonist, of Mira, her long dead mother-in-law and of Kalpana, a rape victim. The novel unfolds the grief of Urmila over the death of her infant child. She encounters the diaries and poems of her dead mother-in-law, reflecting both her suffering and private freedom in her solitude. Then she happens to meet Shakutai, the mother of a rape victim, Kalpana. Through Shakutai, Urmila is able to have some glimpse of the life of the victim. Kalpana is an independent, smart young girl who earns her own money. She wants to get married to the man of her choice. Unfortunately, she is brutally raped by none other than the husband of her mother's sister. She has been in coma since then, struggling between life and death. The protagonist, Urmila finds analogy between the condition of Kalpana and Mira. Both of them were rape-victims, the former, outside marriage and the latter, within marriage. Seeing the suffering of others, helping and sharing their pain, Urmila is finally able to see "the spring of life" and hope, overcoming loss and despair (203).

The next novel, *Small Remedies*, through the protagonist, Madhu, exposes the social and cultural victimization of women and remedies thereof, how women should try to fight against various odds, are suggested. Like *The Binding Vine*, the present novel is about the life of three women—Madhu, Leela (Madhu's aunt) and Savitri Bai Indorekar, a singer on whose life Madhu has to write a biography. Like Urmila, the protagonist is grieving over the death of her only and teenage son, Aditya. Behind this grief-stricken mother, there is a woman in Madhu that has witnessed the disintegration and failure of her relationship with her husband just because of one incident that happened long before, in her life. On the spur of the moment, after her visit to an art exhibition with her husband, much stirred by the sight of a painting painted by one of her father's younger friends causing her a nightmare, she narrated to him how she had come into contact with the man. It was at a time when she was bitterly crying on hearing the news of her father's death that this man (the painter) came right up to her, held her tight in an attempt to console her. Her teenage body, so unused to touch, reacted and responded positively and they ended up in having sex. When her servant came, she had to rush to Bombay where her father's dead body was lying. Her father's death "has blotted out everything else, like a huge cloud it [sic] covers the entire sky" (269), and she forgot the incident in due course until she saw the painting of this man who had committed suicide because of the guilt, because of what he had done to her. Her relationship with Som, her husband, has changed ever since the day she disclosed the story.

> But it is the single act of sex that Som holds on to, it's this fact that he can't let go of, as if it's been welded into his palm. Purity, chastity, an intact hymen—these are the things Som is thinking of, these are the truths that matter. (262)

Here, the novelist, through the character of Madhu, seems to put forth the importance attached to women's virginity by men. For him it is female virginity, chastity, the pure sexual body of a woman that counts, and nothing else as far as man-woman relationship is concerned. The novelist seems to criticize typical male attitude toward women as if women were the only custodians of social, moral and sexual codes while they go scot-free. Such attitude of male is found in all societies. Clare in Hardy's *Tess of the D'Urbervilles* no longer loves Tess as he says, "The woman I have been loving is not you"[14] when Tess discloses her past life with Alec, the indication being that it's not Tess, the person Clare had loved but her virginity. In the same way, in Nayantara Sahgal's *Storm in Chandigarh*,[15] Inder cannot accept his wife Saroj's premarital love affair with a boy. Similarly, Som cannot forgive and forget the incident, more so since it was not a case of rape but consensus as Madhu observes:

> I know what the truth is that Som wants from me: that it has not happened, that I was a virgin when he married me. I begin to understand the truth that he could, perhaps, have borne: that I had been raped, forced into the act, that I was a victim, not a participant. (260)

In this context, what Annis Pratt has observed holds true: "Society considers the sex experiences of man as attributes of his general development, while similar experiences in the life of women are looked upon as a terrible calamity, a loss of honour and of all that is good and noble in a human being."[16]

Towards the end of the novel, there is possibility and hope that Madhu will reconcile with her husband as she says "Som and I, we can wash away the darkness and ugliness, not only of Adit's death, but of what happened before, with our own oblations of sesame seeds and water" (323). Finally, she comes to terms with the loss of her only son and attains "some kind of an understanding" that leads her to a harmonious life. "As long as there is memory, there's always the possibility of retrieval, as long as there is memory, loss is never total" (324).

If modern feminist is inclined to humanism, then, Shashi Deshpande is a feminist writer par excellence. In her latest novel, *Moving On,* the height of her understanding of human psyche and delicate emotions is achieved. With this novel, the novelist seems to reach a stage where she treats her characters not merely as men and women but as individual human beings. The themes of alienation, loneliness, emptiness, death, life and hope are dealt with in detail in this novel and these are not only confined to women but also to her male characters. Most of the characters suffer from loneliness, even the most jovial and enthusiastic of them all, including the father of the protagonist who wants to live life to the fullest. Despite these dominant themes, the novelist also manages to bring forth the great disparities between the two genders in our society. In this novel, it is shown through the character of the protagonist how difficult it is for a single woman to live in this male-dominated society. It is also noteworthy how Jiji, the protagonist, faces the various odds and uncertainties of life and hindrances of the society in her own way.

Like the earlier protagonists, Jiji grows up as a fiercely independent woman who knows exactly what she wants and who has no hassles to go for it, even when it's meant to go against her family or the society, for that matter. She is a woman who wants to take hold of the reins of her life to reach the place of her choice as she says; "I want the brakes under my feet, not someone else's. I don't want a dual control, the control should be mine, mine alone"

(88). If "a woman creates her identity by choosing her clothes", or "creates her history by choosing her man,"[17] Jiji is one such woman. If feminism is a matter of freedom of choice making, she is a feminist from the very beginning. Much to the disappointment of her parents who want her to complete her graduation, she has decided to get married to the man of her choice, following her impulse and passion, "It's not Shyam, it's I who don't want to wait. I want him, right now" (187).

The protagonist reacts sharply when her freedom is thwarted. She openly shows her defiance when her mother deliberately does not inform the visit of Shyam, her to-be-husband. Her mother, who is not happy at their relationship, keeps Shyam waiting without informing her. Later when she comes to know about it, she expresses her anger in the following manner:

> The intensity of her disapproval, the relentlessness of her opposition to our relationship surprised me. And angered me, driving me for the first time into opposing her. . . . Realizing what she'd done, I went to him and kissed him on the lips. A brazen declaration, not only of my love for Shyam, but of my defiance of Mai. (186)

It is a wonder when such an outgoing person like her also passes the feminine phase of imitating the customs and conventions of the society. After her husband had committed suicide, feeling guilty of betraying her, she was proposed for marriage by her childhood friend Raja who is also a widower. She frankly tells him, "I don't want to get married, Raja" but carefully holds back, what she actually feels, "I don't mind sex though" thinking "what will he do? What will he say?" (70) It is so unthinkable for Jiji to succumb to 'what people will say?' attitude of most women. When she feels the need to hide her physical relationship with her much younger tenant, Raman from others, especially from Raja, she herself wonders at the kind of person she is becoming as she says:

> I don't go up that night—or the next, or the next. . . . For what? For the possibility that Raja could have seen him, that he might have guessed? Why am I so scared of Raja? (260)

She is constantly struggling to assert herself against the tide of tradition, until at the very end, she is able to overcome everything and be her individual self. When Raja scolds her after finding out the physical relationship she is having with Raman, she unfolds the pain and sufferings she has been bearing all alone in a hostile men's world stoically. She tells Raja that it's her husband who got Malu, her younger sister pregnant, that Sachi is not her daughter but the child Malu had left before she died. She narrates how she had been indecently proposed or suggested for sexual relationship, and how she had been bearing many unwanted sexual advances by various men, including the husband of her friend. She pours out her bitter experiences to Raja:

> What it is for a woman to live alone? I gave up wearing saris because I didn't want to look womanly, I cut my hair short like a man's, I wore my most forbidding expression. But it was of no use. They can smell it, yes, they can smell the woman in you. No matter how you dress, whether you shave your head or hide behind a burkha, they come to you, wanting your body, touching you, drooling over you, sniffing at you. Like dogs. Like dogs in heat. (284)

Here, the novelist seems to portray the insecurity and helplessness of women, who are single in this hostile world of men. This speaks volumes of how women are being victimized at various levels in the patriarchal society. Jiji, after this torrent of words, attains a kind of 'Catharsis' and relieves herself from the long time burden she carries on her shoulder. She is not ashamed of speaking her mind, heart and body. She tells Raja that Raman is decent compared to many others and for her, "it was just his body, nothing but his body" (284). She asserts herself and her sexuality, before she ventures out to a new possible journey with Raja:

> Who am I saying this to? Raja, again Raja. What do I owe him? This is my business, mine alone. I'm doing what I feel like doing and I can put a stop to it whenever I choose to do so. A click of a finger and it's over. (261)

The novel ends with a possibility of Jiji and Raja living together but that's not what is important. This novel, like most of her novels, has an open ending that may lead to various conclusions but what seems obvious is the celebration of selfhood and womanhood by asserting her self, wants and desires on the part of the protagonist.

The latest novel of Shashi Deshpande, *In the Country of Deceit*, is not just another story of adultery, as the underlying current reveals other, deeper aspects of life and relationships. The novel revolves round Devayani or Devi, an educated, middle class woman who had a mind of her own. Unlike Deshpande's earlier protagonists, she was unmarried and much younger (aged 26) yet she had gone through lots of hardships and bore stoically the burden of the family on her young shoulders—her father's death, financial problems, her mother's illness and finally death. She had been confined to Rajnur, a small town, not out of her choice but because of her family's condition. Savitri or Savi, her elder sister, happily married with two kids to her childhood sweetheart, Shree, escaped most of the family problems, physically and mentally, leaving Devayani alone to bear everything. Feeling guilty of her negligence in the family matter, Savi, along with her husband, her aunt, Sindhu (a cancer patient) and her uncle Keshav tried to find 'a suitable boy' for Devayani, but all their efforts were in vain as Devayani was not interested.

All of them were shocked, angry and annoyed when they came to know from Devayani that she's having an affair with a much-married and older man, Ashok Chinnappa, DSP of Rajnur. They could not believe it especially when Devayani told them that she was not cheated, she knew it from the very beginning that he had been married and had a daughter, 10 years old, whom he dearly loved. They were suspicious about the motive of this man mainly because he was a married man. Savi demanded the reason why Devi went down so low to have such meaningless relationship just only for sex. She said, 'I never thought you would do such a dirty thing, just for sex' (184). But the truth was that Devayani had found true love, profound joy and happiness for the first time in her life in this man. Their relationship came to an end as expected but the impact was so great that it would leave a permanent mark not of tragedy but of happiness in Devayani's life. There's no regret.

The novelist's attempt to explore the inner psyche of various women characters, major and minor, deserves special attention. At the same time these bunch of women characters of varied personalities directly or indirectly contribute to the growth and development of her central character, Devayani. One such character was Sindhu who appeared in the novel only through her letters but she occupied a formidable position in the life of the protagonist, not only because she was a surrogate mother but also because of her philosophy and way of life. She advised her to get married not because of any other popular notion attached to it but to avoid loneliness. Having been married twice (the first one was brief as her husband died of illness), she felt that 'being married is a good thing' (26). She was an unconventional lady who had a no-nonsense attitude. She was the one who proposed to Keshav, her second husband. Her views regarding the importance of our body and the need to fulfill its needs were equally untraditional. Through her, Deshpande seems to represent an independent woman who was fearless of what others would say and not acted as expected, ready to defy anything and lived a life of her own. She was one woman who knew her female self without necessarily acting in a certain accepted norm, expressing femininity.

Another woman that draws our attention was Kshama, Devayani's cousin (both Devayani and Kshama had appeared in her earlier novel *Come Up and Be Dead*) who had been a strict principal in a girls' school. She resigned from the post and started a new school of her own in which she took pride. She developed painting as her hobby and sounded happy and excited about it too. Devayani could see a sea change in her overall approach to life and personal relationship. This happy and pleasant woman was quite the opposite of what she had known earlier when she was working as the caretaker of her household. She was always guarded and hostile. She had changed for the better and was ready to make up for her rude behaviour with her. Kshama was more angry and annoyed than grieved at the death of her timid younger brother, Pratap, thinking of its disturbance to her job. Now she realized, 'I find it hard [to] believe I was so callous' (230). Through her character Deshpande seems to suggest the possibility of gearing up our life for better and happier state, putting the bitterness of our failure, personal tragedy and even guilt behind by taking up a profession and a hobby. This was exactly what Devayani was doing at the very end of the novel.

'Rani' or Priya Ranjan and her daughter Roshni—two widely different personalities—were the latest addition to Devayani's life and they too developed a kind of friendship with Devayani. Rani, a former actress who came to Rajnur to settle down with her husband K.N., and children, had a colorful life, quite the opposite to the not-so-happening life of the protagonist. She had been married twice and had a grown up daughter, Roshini, from her first marriage, and another daughter and a son with K.N. In between she had a live-in relationship with a director, Mahesh Tiwari with whom she was madly in love. On Rani's request, Devayani had to provide a story line for her film as Rani wanted to make a comeback to the film world. They even went to meet some director and producer arranged by her former secretary. The meeting was not so fruitful but Devayani could convince them by narrating the script. Rani's elder daughter (from her first marriage), Roshni now a teenager (she still stayed with her father and grandparents at Mumbai) came to visit Rani at Rajnur. Both the mother and the daughter serve as an alter-ego to Devayani. Kusama, her domestic help, was another woman who had full control of her life. She was fearless and frightened of nothing, not even cockroaches, like many other women. Her husband had an affair with a much older woman. But it was she who had walked out on the first time 'he raised his hand against her' (108). Then she decided 'to earn a living as a cook like her mother had done, much to the horror of her brother whose goal in life was to forget the way his mother had earned her money' (109). But she stuck to her decision of making money, at the same time enjoying what she was doing. This woman cooked for Devayani out of loyalty, and accompanied her most of the time at home and sometimes even acting like a guardian.

It is interesting to note how the novelist successfully intertwines the lives of these women, their hopes and despair, pain and suffering, and most importantly how they overcome their fears and failure and get ready to face, live and enjoy life. Deshpande's treatment of her women characters is realistic. She gives them ample freedom for growth in their personality. There was Sindhu, who wanted to explore everything in life as her days were numbered, Kshama changed herself for the better from an irritable, dull and reserved person to the one who took interest in her own school, painting, doing small household things. Rani who used to sit idly, remembering and missing her golden days at filmdom, worked hard, checking out all the possibilities of her own comeback to the film world, willing and excited at the thought of doing a record/cult film, a dream project for her and her lover director. Minor characters like Devayani's mother, Pushpa, who had been living her life for others, finally took up music which she always loved to do, before she died. All these changes in their lives happened with Devayani, the protagonist, at the centre. She too grew as a person—from being a person who followed the pattern of life to an independent one who charted out pattern for herself and finally became a more mature human being.

The importance of self-independence is felt by both minor and major characters in the latest novel too. Devayani was persuaded to stay some more time with them by her aunt till the new house was properly set but she politely declined because she 'was eager and impatient to move in' (7). The urge to stay in one's house symbolizes the search of one's own personal freedom and space. Kshama, her older cousin, proudly showed her tiny apartment, 'such a contrast to the large bungalow she had lived in as the school principal' (229). She was happy there as she said, 'the day I came to live here, I felt at home. I knew this was home. I'd never felt like this before' (229). This celebration of having 'a room of one's own' is required to boost up one's self-independence. For Rani, owning a car and earning money was a sign of both independence and success: 'she'd bought herself a car with the money she got from her first movie' (34).

Like her other novels, Deshpande's belief in life and the need to move on despite everything is quite discernible towards the end of the novel. Obviously Devayani was shattered when her relationship with Ashok came to an end, though it was expected. Physically, she was weak and immobile because of the car accident she and Rani had. She wrote a letter to her aunt Sindhu, confessing everything and felt much better after reading the consoling and comforting reply of her aunt, telling her that life is precious, we should live life to the fullest, making the most of it, as she wrote, 'There is no greater gift than life. I found out when I thought I was close to death, I realized then what life meant' (256). Devayani thought of Rani, consoling her, 'Things pass, Devayani, things change. We lose things, but we also get things we never expected' (242). The kindness, compassion and understanding from unexpected quarters like the stranger, an old woman showing sympathy, and from acquaintance like Iqbal, offering her the much-needed job to work as an assistant to him, made her feel that the world was a nice place to live in. She knew that Ashok would survive as he 'had his work, his ambitions, his dreams for his future life' and 'his love for his daughter' (255). She too had everyone who loved her—her uncle and aunt, her sister and brother-in-law, their children who would visit her soon, then she had her new job to look forward to. She could even feel the presence of the peaceful soul of her parents, satisfied and content to see them happy. Lastly she had those beautiful, unforgettable moments with Ashok which she would treasure without any regret. In fact, she was feeling proud that she too had 'a moment, a very brief moment, when' she raised her arms and fingertips 'brushed the sky' (259), a state of 'supreme happiness, announcing the pinnacle of achievement' (25) that she had always longed for.

The novelist's attempt to discover the journey of a woman's life who was modern in attitude yet grounded, her love and dedication for her families, her love life and sacrifice, her inner psyche, moral fight against right and wrong, her struggle to overcome her guilt, fear and insecurity and at last, her will to move on with life with positive attitude is praiseworthy. The novel is neither just another tragic love-story nor is it about adultery only but the struggle within self and against the forces of ups and downs of life. It also proves that Deshpande's feminism extends to a broader and wider perspective, instead of confining to its narrow concept, embracing all the aspects. The protagonist's self-assertion and self-realisation, at the very end of the novel, seem to reflect the novelist's idea of feminism.

The specialty of the novelist lies in realistic presentation of women's life and their tensions in a male-dominated world and finally, their attempts to come to terms with their problems positively for a better and secure future. Through the characters of the protagonists and the way they finally assert themselves, the novelist seems to clear many notions and misconceptions of most people. In this regard, what Rashmi Gaur has observed holds true to what Deshpande, as a novelist, seems to convey, "the masses, compelled by their habit of reaching at perfunctory conclusions, soon tended to overlook the fact that feminism is much more than a violent whimsical protest by women against everything which has been traditionally associated with them by man."[18]

As discussed already in chapter II, the novelist's main concern is the deconstruction of myths, epics, religious books, the myth of motherhood and the stereotyping of women's image through various mediums. In order to deconstruct these man-made myths, it is necessary to review and reinterpret them to reconstruct the distorted image of women. In her oeuvre, she attempts to focus some of the characters and episodes from the great epics like the *Mahabharata* and the *Ramayana* by bringing women characters and their unspoken feelings and sentiments to the limelight. For instance, in the story, "And What Has Been Decided," the writer successfully reveals the problems and feelings of Draupadi to live with her five husbands. The story also unfolds one very significant insight from the perspective of Draupadi as regards the cause of the great Kurukshetra battle. At the end of the story, Draupadi realized the politics of men by making her believe all the way that the battle was fought because of her:

> It's begun. They are already preparing, they have decided on war, they know there will be war. But why, then, did they not tell me that? Why did they make me believe it is my decision, my doing? Why?[19]

Such path-breaking ideas lead us to think of and review many similar situations where all through the history, literature and even the religious books, women have been made the reason behind all sorts of war and destruction. This blaming game imposed upon women is another widely used means that has been repeatedly exploited by patriarchy. History and fiction had been putting the blame on women for all forms of destruction and war, thereby associating women with vices and negativity. Even today in our day-to-day casual conversation too, such game is played much to the disadvantage of women.

In some cultures, there are popular sayings that all disputes arise because of three 'Ws'—wine, women and wealth. In Kannada too (as quoted by Iqbal Devi's lawyer), 'All crimes are committed for these three things'—land, woman and gold (86). For instance, Eve was held responsible for all kinds of suffering and the downfall of mankind. Even the ten-year-long Trojan War was attributed to the beautiful Queen, Helen. In this connection, what might be proper to say is that these texts were male-written and thus all fault is put on women as the cause of mankind's suffering and nation's destruction. More importantly cultural myths paint her as the root of wars and destruction as if man had not done anything to cause them. Why is Satan not blamed, why not Paris? Women writers like Shashi Deshpande would like to argue that the wars were not so much because of the abduction of either Sita or Helen but because of male pride, which led to such bloody wars and destruction. So women writers often tend to rewrite and deconstruct the cultural myths and male-made history. Through the depiction of Amba, in the story, Deshpande deeply questions and criticizes men's ideas and words as she says, "honour, dishonour, right, wrong—what are these but words used by men to cover their real emotions?"[20] It is apparent that man suffers and lets others suffer to keep his word; Rama had to be sent to the forest for fourteen years because his father had to keep his promise. Feminists ask if Kaushalya had been in the place of Dashrath, would she allow her son Rama to go for fourteen years into exile. The answer is definitely, no.

In all her writings, Shashi Deshpande tries to represent the silence of women's authentic voice. As a novelist, she tries to bring out the real women who have feelings and sentiments in these mythical women like Sita, Draupadi, Kunti, Amba, to name a few. Her position, perhaps, is to deconstruct the idealization of women's image because "it obscures the actual social condition of women and induces them to see consolation in myths rather than work for social change."[21] In a country like India, myths are part and parcel in the everyday life of the people, and hence, the need and importance of reviewing them from the women's perspective is a must.

Shashi Deshpande is bent on deconstructing the myths of marriage and motherhood as well. Marriage has been given too much importance in Indian society so much so that it is marriage that matters more than the partner in most cases as we find in the case of Padmini in *Roots and Shadows*. Marriage occupies a prominent position in her latest novel, *In the Country of Deceit*, as most of the characters seem to have marriage on their mind, searching for a suitable groom for Devayani. It is interesting to note the varied views on marriage by various characters. For a very practical person like Sindhu, marriage, though it was not 'the final solution or even the best' (26), gave company and could avoid loneliness. Having been married twice, she opined that being married was a good thing. According to her, 'Marriage is a gamble. One had to take chance' (26). She stressed on the importance of marriage as a means to fulfill bodily needs and demands because Indian society 'does not allow women to fulfill these desires without marriage' (42-43). Like Padmini in *Roots and Shadows*, Devayani was fed up with other people's queries like, 'when are you getting married?' (15) Moreover she did not believe in getting married for the sake of being married and heading for divorce court. Her uncle, knowing that she was fond of quoting lines of Jane Austen, told her that her heroines got their men at the end. She reasoned that Jane believed in marriage but with the right person. Her sister, Savy's mother-in-law constantly reminded her of her unmarried status and called her 'Bichari.' This reflects our society's attitude to the institution of marriage

Deshpande seems to express her view through the character of Gopal when he says, "Marriage is not for everyone. The demand it makes—a lifetime of commitment—is not possible for all of us"

(69). In India, the divorce rate is still comparatively low in regard to her Western counterparts (though the figure has increased recently) and this does not mean that Indian marriages are more successful and happy. It's because, in most cases, women have to think hundred times before they can think of stepping out of their marriage, even if they have enough reasons to do so. Indian marriage is not only between individuals but also between the families, the communities and relatives, and it makes all the more difficult for women to take the plunge. If the woman is not financially independent, the matter is worst. That's why newly married women have been advised that "a husband is like a sheltering tree." "Without the tree, you're dangerously unprotected and vulnerable. . . . And so you have to keep the tree alive and flourishing, even if you have to water it with deceit and lies" (*That Long Silence*, 32). In this context, Kamala Das's *My Story*, well expresses the plight and predicaments faced by women with unhappy marriage:

> I could not admit to all my marriage had flopped. I could not return home to the Nalapat House, a divorcee, for there had been goodwill between our two families for three generations which I did not want to ruin. . . . My parents and other relatives were obsessed with public opinion and bothered exclusively with our society's reaction to any action of any individual. A broken marriage was as distasteful, as horrifying as an attack of leprosy. . . . I did not have the educational qualifications which would have got me a job either.[22]

For Deshpande, marriage is not made in heaven and there is no mythical or romantic notion attached to it. There is no place for such romantic and fairytale-like ending where boy meets girl, they fall in love and get married and live happily ever after; though most of her protagonists have love marriages. However, the novelist is not against marriage or relationships. The only thing she wishes to present is the realistic picture of the plight and condition of women while trying to fit in in culturally constructed roles assigned to them (that further relegate them) in the name of sacred marriages as well as motherhood. Only the myths and "the movies can elevate marriage to such a pedestal, making it the culminating event of a lifetime, of several lifetimes" (*A Matter of Time*, 65).

Shashi Deshpande, as a novelist, never idealizes women or glorifies the myth of motherhood. In her novels, motherhood is not treated as something sacred or elevated; instead, all the sufferings, inconveniences and pain associated with motherhood are brought forth which had been overlooked in an attempt to glorify it. As the narrator of the novel, *If I Die Today,* expresses, "Motherhood, I thought. It's a trap. Keeping you in cage until you lose the desire for freedom; until you forget what the word 'freedom' means."[23] Sindhu's views regarding motherhood and parenting reflect Deshpande's own attitude towards these topics. In one of her letters to Devayani, Sindhu shares her joy and excitement at getting the first grandchild and at the same time, gives a realistic, not the idealistic version of it as she says, 'I've heard so many stories about being a grandparent, and most of them are true, but the one thing no one told me about is how tiring it is!' (17). Parenting, according to her, is an 'exhausting and thankless job' (18). The novelist doesn't believe in the idealization of motherhood and hence, her mothers are not always good, perfect and sacrificing. This may be a subtle suggestion that too much expectation from mothers is not desirable as they are also human beings who have their own individuality, weakness and strength.

The glorifying image of motherhood has been created and promoted by various forms of art, literature, paintings, myths, religion and even in entertaining industries like films. When Napoleon Bonaparte said the much quoted line, "Give me a good mother, I will give you a good nation," the image of a kind, loving, ever-forgiving, ever-sacrificing mother who has to sacrifice practically everything comes into the picture. However, nobody—great men or ordinary people—seem to bother or expect the same thing from fathers. "Like all military men, Napoleon preferred to see in woman only a mother,"[24] but the truth is that woman is not only a mother but also an individual. It is not only military men but also men from all spheres who prefer to put the burden on women, which they themselves are not willing to carry. These burdens are so beautifully and carefully wrapped and decorated with the tradition and honour that women themselves begin to take them as compliments but not as burdens on them. In this way, women have been fooled and they have been living in fools' paradise for ages. Even in this modern age, where both men and women are working, the same expectation from women is still there. Child-rearing and household chores are still considered to be her duties only.

As a writer, Deshpande tries to expose the reality rather than the myth of motherhood. Most of her protagonists like Urmila, Saru, Jaya, Jiji, no doubt, love their children but they do not fit themselves to the celebrated roles of motherhood as mentioned in chapter II. Asked why the mothers in her novels are so unloving, Deshpande answers:

> Unloving? No, it's because we have this stereotypical image of what a loving mother is like, that we find any variation to be lacking in 'motherly' feelings. It seems to me that we need to get rid of these images to release ourselves from guilt. (96-97)

Through the character of Gopal, Deshpande in *A Matter of Time*, lays bare the feelings and sentiments of a father that have been always underrated by overrating those of a mother. The novelist emphasizes the need "to set aside all unreal ideas about motherhood . . . to see the vast area of a common ground between fathers and mothers" (97). Despite saying so, Deshpande still feels the need and significance of myths in our day-to-day life. She also points out that myths should not be rejected but should be reinterpreted to keep them still alive and relevant to our present life: "What women writers are doing today is not a rejection of the myth but a meaningful and creative reinterpretation of them."[25]

Female sexuality is another very significant attempt made by the novelist. Deshpande's daring exploration of women's bodies and sexualities is the direct manifestation of denial of masculine dictates towards women. She challenges the age-old notion that woman should hide her sexuality if she has any, as if it's a shameful thing. She seems to agree with Helene Cixous when she says that woman has to "Speak of her pleasure . . . so that she gets to unblock a sexuality that's just as much feminine as masculine."[26] Her protagonists are sexually aware of their bodies, wants and desires. Women in the creation of men are vamps, wanton women or women who have no such desires at all. Between these two extremities lie Deshpande's protagonists. They no longer think "sex" as a taboo but rather take it as one of the physical needs to be fulfilled and satisfied "like drinking water when you're thirsty" (*Moving On*, 259).

In *Roots and Shadows*, the novelist describes the physical relationship between Indu and Naren (which is outside marriage) as "pure sanctity and solemnity." Here "sex is not taken as something dirty when two persons are willing or loving it" (160). The protagonist, Indu, asserts her sexuality as part of her individuality. Saru, in *The Dark Holds No Terrors*, is described as "a physically aroused woman, with an infinite capacity for loving and giving with a passionate desire to be absorbed by the man" (40) she loved. In *The Binding Vine*, Urmila longed for her husband when he was away. She wished she could put her "desires into a deep freeze and take them out, intact and whole when he returned." She soon realized the only way she "could come to terms with" her "sexuality was to recognize it" (164-65).

In *Small Remedies* too, on their first night, it was Madhu who encouraged Som, her husband, to proceed when he looked hesitated, "It's all right, Som, it's all right. I want it too" (230). In *Moving On*, more stress is given to body and bodily needs by the novelist than she had ever attempted before. Jiji, the protagonist, never associates 'sex' with 'dirtiness' as she thought, "Dirty! My God, it's the most beautiful experience in life—if you love each other, that is" (267). She had no inhibition in owning and showing her sexuality even before and after marriage. She had a satisfying and fulfilling relationship with her husband before he betrayed her and committed suicide:

> I was suddenly hungry for Shyam's body and pulled him on to me. I should have been more circumspect, but the pampering of my body, the massaging, oiling and fomenting it had been given after delivery and the suckling, above all the baby's suckling, the tug at my nipples, had my body come alive. How could I deny it what it wanted? (287)

She even justified herself as regards the physical relation she had with her much younger tenant, Raman, by saying. "The body is honest, yes, it told me its need and I've gone along with it, I've done nothing wrong?" (259)

The theme of female sexuality is fully explored in the novel, *In the Country of Deceit* too through the characters of Devayani and Sindhu especially. Devayani's relationship with Ashok is based on love and honesty and they're mutually attracted to each other. Their relationship embraced everything including sex as she said, 'Yes, more than joy. Bliss. And he could give it to me with a touch, with a word. It was this man, not the sex. This man's love, not the sex. And yet, the sex too' (193). What is noteworthy here is the novelist's treatment of sex. It is neither treated as a taboo nor a dirty thing, nor as something that needs to be hidden as Devayani rightly observed, 'How can you not long for the physical union? . . . It's the desire for union, the most complete union two human beings can achieve' (226). Sindhu, in her letters, stressed the importance of the body and the need to fulfill its demand. She took it as a natural feeling. She referred to the word 'ananda,' quoting from the *Upanishad*, to describe the physical pleasure. She told Devayani: 'Remember, this is a very natural feeling, a very natural desire and you have a right to expect your life to contain this ananda as well' (43).

By presenting the sexuality of women without any inhibition, Shashi Deshpande seems to explore two very important aspects of feminism. One, she challenges the stereotype image of women very often found in the fiction of most men writers, making them shy, docile, passive in matters of sex and also attacks the traditional belief that women had no passion and hence could not experience orgasm. Second, as a woman writer, her freedom of expression regarding women's sexuality and anatomy in a very frank manner undoubtedly crosses the man-made boundaries and enters the domain that had been considered exclusively for male writers till recently. It is not so easy even in this modern age for a woman writer to write about sex and passion very explicitly. However, some women writers like Shashi Deshpande, Shoba De, Anita Desai, Kamala Das and Arundhati Roy, to name a few, successfully explore the theme as openly as their male counterparts, claiming their rights as writers and individuals too. This is another way of deconstructing the patriarchal system.

One very important aspect presented by the novelist is the use of women as agents to further propagate patriarchal concepts/ regime by conditioning women to internalize the concepts and use them against themselves. This is a kind of 'divide and rule' policy of the sexual politics played by patriarchy to forever relegate women and colonize them as a group. To use one woman against another is perhaps, the best tool designed by the system: "women must know fear" (*The Binding Vine*, 148), "women should not have any pride" (*A Matter of Time*, 161), "a husband is like a sheltering tree," "If your husband has a mistress, or two, ignore it; take up a hobby instead—cats, may be, or your sister's children" (*That Long Silence* 32, 31). So many 'dos' and 'don'ts,' 'should' and 'shouldn't' are still propagated by women to women from generation to generation, failing which women have to face dire consequences. Such underlying and complex layers of sexual politics are exposed brilliantly by the novelist.

The ironically paradoxical situation where women characters stand in the way of women while some men characters are shown supporting and helping women out of the clutches of the exploited condition to prove their worth is another significant exposition of the novelist that deserves to be mentioned. To cite a few instances, we have Saru's mother who strongly opposes Saru's idea of studying medicine just because the mother wants to fulfil the responsibility of parents by marrying her off. It is because of her father that Saru is able to pursue the career of her choice and prove her worth as individual. In *Roots and Shadows*, Naren's mother, who was fond of learning music, was strongly discouraged by her mother-in-law, though, her husband supported her. K.M. Pandey rightly observes when he says:

> Through this and other examples Shashi Deshpande conveys an important message that suppression, subjugation and exploitation are not confined to the male-female relationship but exist between a female-female relationship as well.[27]

The same discouragement was there with Savitribai when she wanted to learn music from the women's side. When every possible door was closed to her, it was her father-in-law who let her learn it. He was a liberal man who encouraged girls to go to school, "despite much muttered criticism from the women themselves" (*Small Remedies*, 218). Deshpande, as a novelist, seems to view that women's liberation needs women to exercise goodwill towards other fellow women instead of barring each other's way. She also emphasizes the need to include men to fight for women's emancipation against all forms of injustices and inequalities that affect the life and happiness of both men and women.

The importance and need for female solidarity is another aspect of Deshpande's feminism. Women, as a group, irrespective of class differences, are bound together by some common factors and problems specific to them. These factors can be grouped into two—biological and social. Biologically, they share more or less the same kind of experiences—"puberty, menstruation, sexual initiation, pregnancy, childbirth, and menopause—the entire female sexual life cycle" [28] that bind them together. Socially, they, as a group, suffer under the same system of patriarchy. The need to group together and fight for common cause is a must to generate "a sisterly solidarity, a bond of shared experience, loyalty and compassion."[29]

Women can relate to each other's problems, and together, by sharing and helping each other, they can lighten up their burden even if they fail to solve them. In *That Long Silence*, for instance, Jaya can see and feel the pain and suffering of Nayana, her maidservant, who has been burdened with repeated pregnancies. She notices Nayana's heavily pregnant state and much more while Mohan, her husband, misses all these:

> 'Poor Nayana, pregnant again,' I said to him: but I knew he had noticed nothing, neither Nayana's swollen middle, nor her slim ankles that look so incongruously girlish under that fecund swelling. I saw that and more . . . that the silver anklets which had clinked so gaily while Nayana walked were gone. (8)

In one of their conversations, Nayana talked of her wish to give birth to a son because of a reason quite different from most people, 'Why give birth to a girl behenji, who'll only suffer because of men all her life?' (28) In the same novel, Jaya can relate to the predicament and sufferings of her long-dead mother-in-law who had died after getting aborted. She suffered because of repeated and unwanted pregnancies. Such intimacy with other women, at least, gives solace to each other.

In the novel, *The Binding Vine*, female bonding is one of the dominant themes taken up by the novelist. As Indira Nityanandam observes, "the step forward achieved in this novel, is the introduction of female bonding, the desire of one woman to help another less fortunate one."[30] The novel unravels the grief and sorrow of the protagonist, Urmi, over the death of her baby daughter. There's Vanaa, her childhood friend, and her mother and other family members who take care of her and try to bring her back to her normal self. However, it is the sudden discovery of her late mother-in-law Mira's poems and diaries and the accidental meeting of Shakutai, the mother of a rape victim, that actually help her in healing her own grief. She can feel and sympathize with her dead mother-in-law and the kind of life she must have experienced. She decides to publish all her poems. The story of Akka, the second wife of her father-in-law, who was married to him just because he needed a mother to his kid son, equally moves her. Urmi tries her best by going out of her way to help the family of the rape victims. She shares their pain and sufferings and tries to persuade them to demand social and legal justice. In this novel, the novelist's attempt to bring 'the binding vine' among her women characters for a better living is quite discernible.

The novelist seems to be preoccupied with the theme of female bonding in *A Matter of Time*. She emphasizes the importance of understanding, compassion and co-operation to lessen each other's loss and despair among women. In this novel, women of three generations have bonded by some common things that happened to them. The three main female figures—her mother Manorama, Sumi, the protagonist, and her eldest daughter Aru—have seen and experienced the disintegration of their families when the male figures had receded themselves from their responsibilities. Monorama and her husband Shripati have not communicated to each other for more than thirty-five years, after he had held her responsible for the loss of their only and handicapped, minor son at a railway station. Monorama, having had the experience of an abandoned wife, worries about her daughter, Sumi, as the latter has been deserted by her husband, Gopal. She even visits Gopal and urges him to come back to his family, "What have you done to my daughter, Gopala, don't do this, don't let it happen to my daughter, what happened to me" (46).

There is Aru who tries her best to bring back her father. From an aggressive teenager, she becomes a sympathetic person towards her mother and grandmother. She focuses on how to make them happy. In the same novel, the bonding between Surekha, a lawyer, and Aru is more than professional. Surekha advises Aru not only as a lawyer but also as a considerate and affectionate sister. She even goes to meet Gopal in an attempt to unite the family to bring back the warmth and security to Aru. Sumi, on her part, bears everything stoically and tries to give happiness and security to her children.

In the later novels, *Small Remedies* and *Moving On*, though it's not the main focus, the theme of female solidarity is not totally missing out. Madhu, who lost her mother very early, does not feel "the lack of a mother" (151) since she has Leela, her mother's sister, with her. Seeing the strong bond between sisters, she wishes to have a sister, "For the first time I wish I had a sister . . . why don't I have a sister?" (151) In the more recent novel, the protagonist, Jiji had a very good rapport with her kid sister, Malu, for whom she was very protective. The theme of sisterhood is very much at the heart of the novel, *In the Country of Deceit*. Almost all the women characters bonded so well, sharing their life, pain, suffering, hopes and aspiration, joy and excitement. The protagonist Devayani had been a caring daughter to her parents, especially her mother, nursing her during her illness, helping Sindhu, her aunt, after the surgery, looking after Kshama, her older cousin, always there for her sister, Savi and family. In turn, they all were there for her to help her, guide her and to pull her out of the chaos and mess she was in, going out of their way, especially her sister, Savi. Rani seemed to find a friend in Devayani and her daughter, Roshni too liked her company. There was some hint of daughter-in-law, mother-in-law not getting along but it was subtle. The overall picture of women characters was of shared love and affection, always ready to help one another. This sisterly love and affection and bonding with another woman is surely a positive step towards the road to a more secure and harmonious life. This is one aspect the novelist seems to underscore. Women's problems and pain can be reduced when they help each other out, instead of engaging in guerilla warfare, always fighting and standing in the way of one another.

Feminism has come a long way and now we have men in feminism and women against feminism. It is because feminism is not against all men but against the system that relegates women as a group. In Deshpande's novels, there are so many men characters who are sympathetic towards women and their problems. If female bonding is one of the aspects of new feminism, the novelist seems to underline the need for male-female bonding as individuals. The men may not necessarily be their father/ husband/ brother; but they may be friends or even acquaintances. As discussed above, there are certain areas where women can share with other women better, but there are so many areas where a man and a woman can share and understand each other too.

For instance, it is men characters like her father and Madhav, at the end of *The Dark Holds No Terrors* that make Saru realize the basic truth about her life and problem. In *Roots and Shadows*, it is Naren, her childhood friend that pulls Indu out to face the reality and see the reason why she's a failed writer. He points out it's because she fights against her womanhood by denying it. His straightforward criticism of her work, that he does not like her stuff because "It has no soul" (77), opens her eyes. She finally, resolves to do the kind of writing she had always dreamt of. In the same way, Kamat, in *That Long Silence*, helps Jaya to see the truth, and face the reality by accepting it and trying to figure out how to change it for the better, in both her personal and professional life. He is the one who helps Mukta, Jaya's neighbour, after her husband's death, as she narrates to Jaya, "after Arun died, it was Kamat who helped me, who gave me the courage to do my teacher's training to take up a job" (185).

In *A Matter of Time*, Sumi does not stop bonding with Gopal, even after he has left her, sharing her worries about their daughter and seeking his advice. When she dies, he too goes and visits his daughters and mother-in-law to share the pain, suffering and the loss together. They, too, in turn, give him support, assurance and sympathy. At the end of the novel, it's nothing but compassion, affection and understanding of one another that finally bind them together. In *Small Remedies*, the protagonist Madhu had a special bond with her father who brought her up single-handedly. She had shared great rapport with other male characters like Joe and Tony, other than her husband. In *Moving On,* too, Jiji, after the death of her parents, sister and husband finds compassion and consolation in the company of her childhood friend, Raja. The novelist through her novels seems to show that if women have to find happiness and freedom, they need to bond with not only themselves but also with men.

Another important exposition of the novelist is the male chauvinism prevailing in the society with a critical view of the same. In *Roots and Shadows*, Indu was consoled and advised by her old uncle in a worldly-wise and experienced manner: "We like our women not to think" (33). This is a frank, straightforward and candid kind of confession revealing the dominating and superior attitude of men to relegate women to her domestic sphere. In *That Long Silence* too, when Ramakaka excitedly showed their family tree that went back for nearly two hundred years, Jaya noticed the absence of all women who had been married off and married to the family. She was shocked to find no place for her and all the women who had been toiling and sacrificing all their lives for the sake of thc family.

When Mira, in *The Binding Vine*, showed some of her poems to the well-known poet, Venu, whom she admired greatly, he said, "Why do you need to write poetry? It is enough for a young woman like you to give birth to children. That is your poetry. Leave the other poetry to us men" (127). It reflects the typical, age-old male's attitude that cannot associate women with poetry or creativity. In *Small Remedies* too, when Savitribai Indorekar, after crossing all barriers, came to her music Guru, he refused several times before he finally agreed, thinking, "music was no profession for a respectably married woman. Because he, a traditional man, did not want to encourage her to step out of her traditional role" (130).

In *Moving On*, when the instructor praises her driving capability, "Madam, you are not like other women" (84), he is simply repeating the same old male chauvinism that tends to associate such practical and smart things only with men. In the same novel, while trying to search for a particular place, she asks Raja about it, and finding him confused, she decides to find it herself anyway. Through the words of Jiji, Shashi Deshpande seems to criticize and challenge the stereotypical concepts and views of men towards women, as she says:

> More and more as I live, I realize that the belief that men know better, that they are better at practical details, is an illusion. I think of Gayatri, Kamala, Mai and all the women of their times deferring to male opinion in matters outside the home. Did they, even after losing faith in the greater sagacity of men, go on pretending in the interest of domestic peace? (179)

Deliberate gender role reversal is another feminist concern explored by Shashi Deshpande in her novels. Here, the idea is to challenge the rigid norms of patriarchal society by masquerading the masculine traits. In *Roots and Shadows,* Indu's Akka who had been forcibly married to a much older man of past thirty, suffered greatly in her married life. Many-a-time, she had tried to run away but was caught and locked up in a room and kept there for days without food. After "fifteen or twenty years, he took up with one woman" (70). He had a stroke and he wanted his mistress but Akka did not allow him to meet her, taking her sweet revenge of her long suffering at his hands. She says:

> Listen to me. It's my turn now. I've listened to you long enough. She came here. Twice, she wanted to see you. She cried and begged to be

> allowed to see you just for a short while. I threw her out. You'll never see her again. (71)

Here, she became the master, holding and exercising the complete control of his life. In most cases, it is men who use women for their advantage but the novelist makes her women use men as a means to further their career or satisfy their needs. For instance, Savitribai Indorekar in *Small Remedies* used Ghulam Saab and the station Director of the radio station in Neemgaon to further her singing career. In the same way, Saru in *The Dark Holds No Terrors* uses Boozie for her medical career. In *Moving On*, it is the protagonist Jiji who directs and controls the physical relationship between her and her younger tenant by setting rules:

> He can never come to my house, it is I who will go to him. He can never approach me, he can never ask me any question. He has to wait for me to go to him, the decision will be mine, mine alone. He has to accept this. (258)

Here, the novelist's attack on the patriarchal norms is not by contrast but by ambivalence by employing gender role reversals deliberately.

Another very significant aspect of the novels of Shashi Deshpande is the realization of acute sense of victimization of women at the hands of patriarchy. The conditions of women and their position both in and outside the domestic walls are still deplorable, though there are some outward changes recently. Social, cultural, religious and traditional norms still manage to relegate women to a secondary position even in this modern age. Even intelligent and well-qualified women are treated as puppets in the name of guarding family's honour and tradition. In most cases, their acquisitions are taken for granted. Their most important decisions of life are generally taken by their parents before marriage, by their husbands after marriage and by their sons when they are old, still religiously following what Manu had dictated many centuries before:

> Day and night, women must be kept in subordination to the males of the family, in childhood to her father, in youth to her husband, in old age to her sons.[31]

Such attitude and notion clearly indicate that women are incapable of taking decisions of their own life and hence, should remain under the supervision of males throughout their life. In this way, women have been denied many opportunities that men have been enjoying since time immemorial and therefore, chances to prove their worth are ruled out in most cases.

Deshpande's novels emphasize that a woman, besides being a daughter, a wife and a mother, is also a human being, an individual that has the need for self-fulfillment and self-actualization. They become aware of their self and also the society's biased treatment of women. This is a passing but a necessary phase of their struggle to prove themselves. The protagonists of Deshpande strive to overcome their identity crisis by searching for their own identities and the meaning of their life. They become rebels against those dominating forces, and finally they are able to overcome everything by liberating themselves.

As a novelist, Shashi Deshpande is one of those few women writers who do not succumb to the extreme attitude that women-are-always-victims, as she is able to see men are also, sometimes, very much victims of their own system as women are. For instance, Manohar in *The Dark Holds No Terrors* becomes a sadist from being a loving and caring husband to Saru because of the system of the society where men are expected and supposed to be always superior to women. In *Roots and Shadows*, too, through the character of Hemant, the novelist seems to opine that it is not only women but also men who feel tied down and trapped by marriage as he confides to Indu, "The way these women pestered me to get married to them! It's a trap . . . that's what marriage is" (60). In the same novel, Indu's Kaka, "even after becoming a grandfather, could be reduced to a red-faced shuttering schoolboy by Akka's venomous tongue!" (22) In *That Long Silence*, too, it was Jaya's "other ajji" who dominated and ruled over her family.

By projecting some of her male characters as victims and some women characters as dominating, Shashi Deshpande not only reflects a part of reality in the society but also points out the blind spot in the writings of most women writers that have a tendency to turn blind to anything that is good in men and bad in women. They seem to look in every woman, a victim, and in every man, a predator. The novelist seems to be aware of the possible danger of such an extreme view and she is able to avoid it by treating both her men and women characters objectively. Ever since the arrival of feminist criticism on the literary scene, men's writings have been criticized and scrutinized for their inauthenticity and incompleteness in portraying women characters. As Virginia Woolf has rightly pointed out, the unrealistic presentation of women by men writers, "until very lately women in literature were the creation of men,"[32] if women writers too use the same defective weapons against men by creating men characters with only their ugliness, by exaggerating their faults and overlooking their goodness, there is danger of repeating the same mistake committed by men writers regarding women characters. To avoid such inauthenticity in the writings of women, there is need to treat both men and women characters objectively though the focus may be on the latter. This is exactly what is found in Shashi Deshpande's oeuvre.

Deshpande, as a novelist, rejects the masculine concept and tradition of writing. In her writings, we find an authentic female voice, that has no fear in speaking out her body and mind in the language of her own. In this context, what Rashmi Gaur has observed deserves some attention:

> Deshpande's narratives bear the authenticity of a woman's signature. She has rejected the masculine dialect and the masculine perception of virtue, relationship and content, and laid bare before us the subversive role of tradition in perpetuating the secondary role of women, emphasizing the need of discrediting its legacies if women have to emerge as liberated and emancipated beings.[33]

Lastly, Deshpande's feminism, as reflected in her novels, is never against motherhood, the institution of marriage, family, society, men, religion but against the system, idealization and monopolization that work together against man-woman relationship by creating wide gap between them. Her feminism is meant to improve man-woman relationship in the family and society that should be based on mutual co-operation and understanding. Women's victimization will come to an end only when men and women join hands to discard all those inequalities and injustices prevailing in the society. Women are not only daughters, mothers and wives but also human beings who need to prove themselves, like men. Once more Deshpande's ideas of feminism may be seen in their own dynamic nature, not one-sided anti-man like the Western feminist position:

> Is to be a feminist to want to be like a man? I don't think so. On the contrary, to me it has meant an acceptance of my womanhood as a positive thing, not as a lack. An understanding that I am different, not inferior. And how can feminism be anti-men when it is really working for a better, a more meaningful and companionable relationship between man and woman, instead of the uneasy relationship between tyrant and oppressed? . . . I believe that the family is not a divine, sacred institution, but one created by humans for the benefit of all society; and therefore, it should be built, not on the sacrifice of some, but on the co-operation and compromises of all its members. The loud cry of the new-born is a triumphant assertion of being—I AM. Does a baby girl cry less loudly?[34]

NOTES

1. Shashi Deshpande, "Why I am a Feminist" *Writing from the Margin and Other Essays* (New Delhi: Penguin India, 2003), 83.
2. *Ibid.*, 82.
3. *Ibid.*, 84.
4. Ranjini Jyothi Singh, "Quest for Space and Selfhood in Shashi Deshpande," *Pegasus—A Journal of Literary and Critical Studies*, Vol. IV, Jan.-Dec. 2005: 25.
5. Geeta Gangadharan, "Denying The Otherness" (Interview) R.S. Pathak, ed., *The Fiction of Shashi Deshpande*, 252.
6. K. Meera Bai, "The Non Conformist," *Women's Voices: The Novels of Indian Writers* (New Delhi: Prestige, 1996), 61.
7. C.G Jung, *Aspects of the Feminine*, trans. R.F.C. Hull (London: Routledge and Kegan Paul, 1982), 45.
8. Qtd Satish C. Aikant, "Culture and Decolonization," Satish C. Aikant, ed., *Critical Spectrum: Essays in Literary Culture,* (Delhi: Pencraft, 2004), 73.

9. Y.S. Sunita Reddy, *A Feminist Perspective on the Novels of Shashi Deshpande*, 157.
10. S.P. Swain, "*Roots and Shadows*: A Feminist Study," R.S. Pathak, ed., *The Fiction of Shashi Deshpande*, 95.
11. Simone de Beauvoir, "Situation: The Married Women" *The Second Sex*, 426.
12. Shirin Kudchedkar, "Feminist Literary Criticism: The Ground Work," *Journal of Literary Criticism*, Vol. VIII, No. 1, June 1996: 33.
13. Nirmala Prakash, "From Feminine to Feminist Consciousness: Shashi Deshpande's *The Stone Women*," T.M.J. Indra Mohan, ed., *Shashi Deshpande: A Critical Spectrum* (New Delhi: Atlantic, 2004), 29-30.
14. Thomas Hardy, *Tess of the D'Urbervilles* (Rpt. London: Macmillan, 1949), 293.
15. Nayantara Sahgal, *Storm in Chandigarh* (London: Chatto and Windus, 1969).
16. Annis Pratt, *Archetypal Pattern in Women's Fiction* (Bloomington: Indiana University Press, 1981), 37.
17. Elaine Showalter, "Towards a Feminist Poetics," Mary Jacobus, ed., *Women Writing and Writing about Women*, 31.
18. Rashmi Gaur, "The Feminine Perspective in Virginia Woolf," *Women's Writing: Some Facets* (New Delhi: Sarup, 2003), 1.
19. Shashi Deshpande, "And What Has Been Decided," *Collected Stories*, Vol. 2, 245.
20. "The Inner Rooms," *The Intrusion and Other Stories*, 99.
21. Cheri Register, "American Feminist Literary Criticism: A Bibliographical Introduction," Josephine Donovan, ed., *Feminist Literary Criticism: Explorations in Theory* (Kentucky: University Press of Kentucky, 1975), 6.
22. Kamala Das, *My Story* (New Delhi: Sterling, 1976), 108-9.
23. Shashi Deshpande, *If I Die Today* (New Delhi: Vikas, 1982), 47.
24. Simone de Beauvoir, *The Second Sex*, 110.
25. Shashi Deshpande, *Writing from the Margin and Other Essays*, 99-100.
26. Helene Cixous, "Castration or Decapitation?" ed. Mary Eagleton, *Feminist Literary Theory: A Reader*, 322.
27. K.M Pandey., "Tearing the Veil: *The Dark Holds No Terrors*," R.S. Pathak, ed., *The Fiction of Shashi Deshpande*, 52.

28. Elaine Showalter, "A Literature of Their Own: British Women Novelists from Bronte to Lessing," Mary Eagleton, ed., *Feminist Literary Theory*, 17.
29. Qtd Elaine Showalter, "Towards a Feminist Poetics" Philip Rice and Waugh, ed., *Modern Literary Theory: A Reader.* 96.
30. Indira Nityanandam, "Shashi Deshpande's *The Binding Vine*: Silent No More," R.K. Dhawan, ed., *Indian Women Novelists,* Set III, Vol. 4 (New Delhi: Prestige, 1995), 66.
31. Qtd M. Mani Meitei, "Feminism and Anita Desai's *Cry, the Peacock* and *Where Shall We Go This Summer*?" P.M. Nayak and S.P. Swain, ed., *Feminism and Indian Fiction*, 45.
32. Virginia Woolf, "Women and Fiction," *Granite and Rainbow* (London: The Hogarth Press, 1958), 82.
33. Rashmi Gaur, "Images of Indian Woman in Shashi Deshpande's *That Long Silence*: Stereotypes, Myths and Realities," *Women's Writing: Some Facets*, 67.
34. Shashi Deshpande, *Writing from the Margin and Other Essays*, 83-84.

Problems and Predicaments Faced by Women

Here in this chapter, the problems and predicaments that Shashi Deshpande's women characters face will be discussed under four sub-headings: the first will focus on the common problems shared by all sections of women, irrespective of difference in caste, class or creed, binding them together under the same umbrella of having been born women; the second being those problems peculiar to the educated working class women; the third will to examine those problems faced by lower class, illiterate women, and the fourth emphasizes those individual problems faced by various women that may not be generalized. An in-depth study of these problems each in turn will be made as under: Common problems faced by women in the novels of Shashi Deshpande.

There are two classes of women in Deshpande's novels—the educated, modern, usually working women, and the illiterate, traditional (in outlook), lower class women—who suffer by virtue of their sex in a patriarchal society. From time immemorial, women have been treated as inferior to men in almost all societies, East or West. In such religious scripts as *The Bible*, Eve is said to have been created out of the supernumerary bone of Adam. Aristotle believed: "The female is a female by virtue of a certain lack of qualities" and St. Thomas regarded woman as "imperfect man," an "incidental"[1] being. Similarly, Descartes, Dante and Shakespeare treated women as inferior to men. What is apparent is the sexual discrimination exercised by the patriarchal society against women for centuries. This means women's marginalization and victimization in the male-centred culture, where women have lost their voice, and their roles having been fixed or presented already. As

Simone de Beauvoir says: "One is not born, but rather becomes, a woman."[2]

The novelist also reveals the society's preference for the male over the female child and its unhealthy impact on the minds of girl children and their mothers. During the period between 1978-1983:

> 78,000 female foetuses were aborted. Out of 12 million girls born in India every year, one-fourth die before they are 15. One-sixth of those deaths are due to sex determination . . . abortion of female foetuses is increasing alarmingly.[3]

Many studies and researches conducted in various parts of the world prove that the preference is almost universal, though seemingly it is more strongly felt here, in India. In Hindu religion, it is believed that the birth of the son will free the father of all the sins committed. The novelist points out that women have been trained at family level for future unequal and biased treatment in the larger social arena. In *The Dark Holds No Terrors,* Saru, the protagonist of this novel, poignantly recalls that there was no special celebration of her birthday like that of her brother. As a child, Saru suffered emotionally and mentally when everyone, especially her mother, showered all her love and affection upon her son. Such a gender divide that ultimately leads to women's sense of sexual discrimination has affected women's life, in general, right from their childhood.

In *The Binding Vine*, Vanna is neglected by her father while his attention and affection are directed towards his only son, Kishore. To her father, she is as it were non-existent; she fails to draw her father's attention even if she tries to do so by laughing rather too long, but alas the former remains quite indifferent to his daughter, much to the shock of Vanna. For him, there was only his son, Kishore. Urmila, the central character, heard Vanaa say once that her father expected nothing from her. Maybe he neglected her because he had been extremely obsessed with his first wife, hence his obsession with her son only. In *Roots and Shadows* too, Indu, the protagonist, wondered whether her father would have been more attentive if she were born a son. She was with her grandparents after her mother's untimely death, and her father hardly visits her. She recalls:

> How else could he have parted leaving me a fifteen-day-old motherless baby, with the family he hated and despised? He had not even come to see me until I was more than a year old. But that, perhaps, was because I was a girl. If I had been a son . . . (163)

Importance given to the male members of the family in our society is also exposed in the latest novel of Deshpande. Devayani's grandfather neglected her mother, Pushpa who had been suffering from epilepsy in the beginning because she was a daughter, not a son. Later on, he regretted as he wrote to his friend, "If Pushpa had been a son instead of a daughter, would I have behaved in the same way? The answer I got is 'no'" (103). Her grandfather's attitude is very common in Indian society but not everyone realizes the mistake. He gave her education by keeping a tutor at home and gifted her a vast land in an effort to make up for his earlier negligence. From the very beginning till the present age, man has been enjoying every privilege at the cost of woman. Sindhu rightly pointed out that in all cultures, be it Christianity or Hinduism, one thing remained the same, despite varied theories of the origin of mankind, that it was man who was believed to have been created first and then came woman, sealing permanently the primary position of man. She cited example from the *Bible* of how Eve was created from Adam's ribs and compared it with the creation story from the *Upanishad* that says, 'First there was one, he wanted another and split himself into two' (97). She noticed that 'even here the first individual is a 'he,' and the 'she' comes later (97). Her observation is noteworthy as she pointed out that man, from the very beginning created stories to enhance their superiority to woman.

In India a son is always rated very high, even mothers of sons are given an honour by the society. Monorama, in *A Matter of Time*, who came from a poor family, earnestly wanted a son to prove her worth, but was deeply disappointed when a daughter was born instead. To her, her daughter became the visible symbol of her failure. Again Jaya, in *That Long Silence*, remembered how her mother's love, affection and care, 'swarming' over her brother but not giving much attention to her. Here is a blood-curdling account of Jaya as regards the fate of girl children:

> Where was it I had read an account of how baby girls were done to death a century or so back? They were, I had read in horror, buried alive, crushed to death in the room they were born in; and immediately after that, a fire was lit on the spot—to purify the place, they said. Perhaps it was to ensure death. . . . But now I wondered whether it wasn't more merciful, that swift ending of the agony once and for all, than this prolonging of it for years. (53)

When girls grow up and get married, there is still no end to their problems. When Indu speaks of her childhood experience with so many restrictions, so many 'do's' and 'don'ts,' she reminds us of every girl child's precarious life in store for her:

> As a child, they had told me I must be obedient and unquestioning. As a girl, they had told me I must be meek and submissive. Why? I had asked. Because you are a female. You must accept everything, you are a girl. . . . It is the only way, they said, for a female to live and survive. (158)

In this connection, one can see the painful life of a woman in a culture where she is dictated to be faithful, obedient and conformist. As Kamala Das says in "An Introduction":

> Dress in sarees, be girl,
> Be wife, they said. Be embroiderer, be cook,
> Be a quarreler with servants. Fit in. Oh,
> Belong, cried the categorizers. Don't sit
> On walls or peep in through our lace-draped windows. [4]

This is how women have been trained and convinced that their sex is not separate from gender. The matter that sex is biologically determined whereas gender is culturally given has been kept confused by Patriarchy, so that every female is essentialiy feminine and that is biologically given. It is sexism that downplays women in order that man continues to enjoy a privileged position while woman's suffering perpetuates. It is in this way that women have been trained from a young age to behave in a certain way which feminists tend to oppose. Such dichotomous attitudes and divide between man and woman in the society are quite discernible in Deshpande's oeuvre.

No wonder, such a society does not permit a girl to choose her spouse independently. If, on the contrary, a girl chooses her spouse, she runs the risk of disobeying her parents. In such cases, girls have to pay a heavy price. They are no longer welcome to their own house. In *The Dark Holds No Terrors* when Saru decided to marry Manohar, the man of her choice, her mother said, "I know all these 'love marriages.' It's love for a few days, then quarrels all the time. Don't come crying to us then." (69)

Talking about marriage, it would not be wrong to say that marriage, to most Indian women—educated or uneducated, rich or poor, high class or low class—means a change of surname, habits, attitudes, identity, personality, lots of sacrifice, surrender, adjustment and sometimes, even change of names. In India too, much importance is given to the institution of marriage as studied in earlier chapters. Padmini in *Roots and Shadows* was ready to get married to any man who said 'yes' since she could not afford to repeat the hectic and difficult process of fixing up an engagement as she confides to Indu:

> Any man, Indu? Yes any man. Any man who says "yes." You don't know what it has been like. Watching Kaka and Hemant and even Madhav-Kaka running around after eligible men. And then, sending horoscope and having it come back with the message, "It doesn't match." And if the horoscopes matched, there was the meeting to be arranged. And Mother and Atya slogging in the kitchen the whole day. And all those people coming . . . and staring and asking all kinds of questions. And if we heard they were old fashioned people, I would dress up in an old fashioned manner and they would say, "She's not modern enough." And if I dressed up well because someone said the boy wanted a smart wife, they would say, "She's too fashionable for us." Or too short. Or too tall. Or too dark. Or something. And Kaka trying to laugh and talk to those people, while his eyes looked so . . . anxious. And I, feeling as if I had committed a great crime by being born a girl. To make your parents look like that. . . . And then, they would say, someone else in the family wants to see the girl. So we would have to go through it all over again. And finally, if everything was fine, there was the dowry. You know noth-

> ing of this, Indu. And now, when someone has agreed, can I refuse and make Kaka go through all of it all over again? Just because the man isn't . . . (126)

She further told Indu that she could no longer bear to hear from anyone saying about it anymore "'How old are you? And not married yet! What a pity!' I'm tired, Indu I don't care what kind of a man he is. Once we are married and he becomes my husband, none of his flaws will matter" (126). In India, most women are left with practically no choice in everything, including those important decisions of life as Kalindi Muzumdar points out: "The family, community and society in general assume that women have to be told, nay ordered to behave in accordance with the norms of the family, community and society. The average Indian woman has no choice in relation to important events in her life such as marriage, parenthood, family planning, participation in community activities and divorce."[5]

After marriage, it is generally the women who have to adjust and sacrifice many things, sometimes even their names and career, to be accepted, loved and admired by their husbands and in-laws. Changing of one's name after marriage as per the wishes of one's husband and in-laws is very common in Indian society. Urmila in *The Binding Vine* recalled what her grandfather had said about the importance of people's names:

> People's names are very important, he used to say. You shouldn't take liberties with them. It is funny, because his wife, my Baiajji, systematically took people's names away from them. Maybe because she had lost her own. I never knew her name was Kamala; everyone, even Papa, called her Bai. (119)

Smita in *The Dark Holds No Terrors* has changed her name, now she is called 'Geetanjali' or 'Anju' according to the wish of her husband. He gets very annoyed if anyone calls her Smita. In *That Long Silence*, too, the protagonist's name was changed from 'Jaya,' given to her by her father at the time of her birth, to 'Suhasini' given by her husband at the time of their marriage. There seems to have been a drastic change in almost everything including the names and identities between the life before and after marriage for women as if marriage is a second birth for them. Mira in *The Binding Vine* was called "Nirmala' after her marriage much against her own wish as we find in her poem:

> Nirmala, they call, I stand statue-still.
> Do you build the new without razing the old?
> A tablet of rice, a pencil of gold
> Can they make me Nirmala? I am Mira. (101)

This shows woman is a territory to be conquered and named by man—a traditional position of woman in a highly genderized world. Man uses woman as his property, observes Simone de Beauvoir. Nirupa Rani goes on to say, "A woman is like a man's land and land is power and property."[6] Men have every advantage to mould and use women to satisfy their whims and fancies. Women have been taught that "a husband is like a sheltering tree" even if he is a drunkard and has mistress, he must be worshipped like god because without that tree, they would be "dangerously unprotected and vulnerable" (32). Mohan's mother in *That Long Silence* waited on her drunken husband however late he was. After giving dinner to her children, she again had to cook rice for him because he wanted his rice "fresh and hot, from a vessel that was untouched." She waited hoping that he would come soon before the rice got cold. It was unthinkable to light the fire again. He came after a long wait, and complained that there was no 'fresh chutney' (35). The next moment he picked up his heavy brass plate and threw it at the wall, and walked out of the house. Disturbed by the noise, two of her older children woke up, but she told them to sleep, saying it's nothing. She asked the boy to go to the next-door neighbour to ask for some chilies. She lighted the fire again with the wood that was difficult to burn. Her eyes were red with the smoke. Meanwhile her baby woke up and cried. She hushed it by feeding. Mohan narrated the above story to his wife, Jaya. She found the story painful and he commented that women in those days were tough. Jaya reacted:

> He saw strength in the woman sitting silently in front of the fire, but I saw despair. I saw despair so great that it would not voice itself. I

> saw a struggle so bitter that silence was the only weapon, silence and surrender. (36)

Here, Mohan's mother had to suffer in silence as if it's nothing when everything went so wrong. Such is not an isolated case; millions of women face this problem everyday in Indian society. Suffering, silence and surrender are part of life of higher middle class women, no matter how educated they are. Always we know that Jaya has to suffer like the mythical women, Sita, Savitri, Draupadi, Gandhari etc. when her husband is accused of business malpractice. Mohan thinks that his wife would share in his fall.

Another aspect of marriage is the eventual loss of women's identity. It seems women have surrendered their identity in their families at their husbands' place. As if they had nothing to contribute, they are always excluded from important discussions. In *Roots and Shadows*, even the most powerful woman, Akka, has not been given a place of her own during family discussions. As has been pointed out in the earlier part of the discussion, women are insultingly removed from the family tree as Jaya sees and reacts in *That Long Silence*. What is apparent here is the relegation of women to the margin in the patriarchal society. All this is a testimony to the long suppression of women in patriarchal society. Jaya complains that there is no room for her anger. Saru, too, has her own grievance attached to her sex despite even her position as a medical doctor. This, however, is the common fate of women to which they remain tied; whether it is she or her mother, everything is the same, unalterable. And at the root of everything lies the lack of an independent life of women, even a space to move and act. Jaya applied Virginia Woolf's phrase "a room of one's own" to herself. Saru is here to say, "my mother has no room of her own. . . . And I have so much my mother lacked. But neither she nor I have that thing a room of our own" (135-36).

In *Moving On,* Jiji's mother who was a writer had to use the dining table to write as the only study table they had was meant for his father. When she was a child, every Sunday, they used to go out with B.K. and Kamala's family. No doubt the husbands enjoyed this outing but they failed to see the boredom and monotony their wives had to bear. To them it was like a punishment. Jiji also recalls that her mother never liked their annual month-long visit to her aunt's place at Bangalore every summer vacation. Her mother did express her discomfort occasionally but nobody cared. These little things of daily life should not be overlooked as ordinary as they might slowly kill the spirit of women when their wishes and interest are repeatedly thwarted. This is the real plight of women in Indian society and Deshpande exposes the injustice done to women.

Deshpande does not stop at that. She brings into light the plight of widows, their hardships and the inhuman treatment meted out to them, evils of child marriage, dowry, and problems of barren women. Women of all classes as a group suffer because of all those expectations, impositions and constructed images created by patriarchy. They have been used, in Virginia Woolf's parlance, as "looking glasses possessing the magic and delicious power of reflecting the figure of man at twice its natural size."[7] Their main problem lies when they fail to do or follow or fulfill these culturally constructed roles assigned to them. In *Roots and Shadows*, Akka was only twelve years when she got married to the man of well past thirty. She became a victim of child marriage. When she refused any intimacy, she was locked up for days without food. The same is the case of Mira in *The Binding Vine*. To them marriage acts like imprisonment, not building a relationship based on mutual love and understanding.

The celibacy of widows is another hindrance in the way of women's emancipation. The novelist gives expression to the harsh reality faced by these women. They have to shave off their heads, wear worn out, old colourless saris, have no possessions and confine themselves in old, shabby rooms. They are made to live a secluded and cut-off life from the society. However, for a widower, everyone—friends, family, relatives—will join hands to search for a new wife as soon as possible. Deshpande speaks of her maternal family in an interview:

> Women have been so indispensable in my mother's family that one could see women dying and immediately the men getting married again. I could see that the female life had no value at all.[8]

This is quite true of Indian society, despite its varied form and regional differences. Here, the novelist has a dig at the social injustice in patriarchal, male-dominated culture of which women are always victims.

Barrenness is another cause of concern and anxiety in the life of women in a society where motherhood is idealized to a great extent. Childless women are looked down upon and treated like sinners and considered as incomplete women. Intelligent and capable women like Indu in *Roots and Shadows* who is childless by choice, and Monisha in Anita Desai's *Voices in the City* have no place and value in the traditional mindset of people who have no regard for women's competence other than bearing and rearing children. As Indu observes, "Nothing about me—my academic distinctions, my career, my success, my money—none of these would impress her. To her I was just a childless woman" (128). Shashi Deshpande depicts the painful and insecure life of childless women. They are often threatened by their husbands as in the case of Shakutai's sister, Sulu, in *The Binding Vine:* "Sulu was frightened; she was always frightened because she had no children. She was afraid he would throw her out, take another wife" (192). Thus the many-layered structure of patriarchal oppression and multiple injury unleashed as women are unfolded by Deshpande in many of her novels.

Still many issues capture the novelist's mind. Women of all classes face the problem of unwanted sex and unwanted pregnancies. Such women who get themselves aborted are scorned by the society. It is because of the general assumption that women are childbearing machines. Repeated pregnancies make them weak and unhealthy. Abortion was considered something shameful and treated as a sin or a taboo. Such a notion is not totally discarded in the present society too. In *That Long Silence,* Monya, Jaya's sister-in-law, narrated to her how her mother had died a week after she got aborted, and how people reacted to it, "People whispered and talked and looked at us oddly. I was ashamed. I knew my mother had done something shameful" (38). On the contrary, how motherhood has been cherished even by eminent personalities like Mother Teresa can be seen when she says:

> God has created women for motherhood. That is the most noble [sic] task. Her place is at home. It is better that she remains at home giving birth to children and rearing them up. Workingwomen are not in a position to bestow attention on their children. . . . Abortion means murder in the womb. There is no greater sin than abortion.[9]

It is at such a moment that the conflict between tradition and modernity comes out. The former trivializes and scandalizes female self-determination by controlling her body. Malladi Subbamma reacts sharply against such misleading and reactionary statement by saying:

> Let us not forget that if women are to confine themselves to the kitchen and the bedroom as per the advice of Mother Teresa, the society will suffer. Even now a woman's life is that of a regulated doll. If Mother Teresa's counsel is to be adopted, a woman will become lifeless. Mother Teresa could receive the Nobel Peace Prize only because she could step out of her house as a nun to serve the people and the orphans in particular. Why did she not live inside the four walls of a house? Why did she aspire to serve God and men by joining the Church? Why did she succumb to the above passionate urge? . . . What is this absurd advice to fellow women?[10]

Of course, that might be relevant in some other context, and perhaps in that context she might have spoken like that. But women-centred views are just the opposite.

Deshpande's heroines tackled the problem of unwanted pregnancies with certain delicacies but with firm determination. As for instance, the protagonist of *That Long Silence* gets herself aborted to avoid unwanted pregnancy. Afterwards, she feels guilty at heart, but no regrets at all. Such feelings are quite normal on the part of the mother. Indu in *Roots and Shadows* asserts herself, "I will have no child that is not wholly welcome" (38). The very fact that they make a choice and decision of their own is, in fact, a step towards women's emancipation that needs to be applauded. The novelist seems to express that women should not be carried away by sentiments and so-called social and moral codes as most of them are constructed much to the disadvantage of women.

An important problem faced by women of all classes is rape within and outside marriage. Rape within marriage is a new concept in Indian society. Saru in *The Dark Holds No Terrors* was subjected to brutal rape every night though she was still the confident doctor with an aura of success during daytime. In this context, what Kate Millet says in *Sexual Politics* is worth mentioning: "The position of women in patriarchy is such that they are expected to be passive, to suffer and to be sexual objects, it is unquestionable that they with varying degrees of success, socialized into such roles."[11]

Her husband, Manohar, was a lecturer in a third-rate college and he could not bear when her wife earned more money and fame than him. Before, he had been a kind and loving husband. He became a sadist when one of the girls who came to interview Saru, asked him, "How does it feel when your wife earns not only the butter but most of the bread as well?'' (200). From that day onwards, he attacked her like an animal just to prove his manhood. Saru had to bear all just to save her marriage.

Similarly, in *The Binding Vine,* Mira and Akka, the first and the second wives of the protagonist's grandfather, were victims of rape within marriage. After the death of Mira, Urmila's grandfather remarried Akka just to provide a mother to his son. Here, the narrator's way of putting the story of Mira and Akka is noteworthy. Shashi Deshpande carefully and successfully juxtaposes by intertwining the story of these two suffering women. Perhaps, the only difference of their suffering might be that Mira suffered because of too much obsessive love of her husband while Akka suffered because of the lack of the same. Urmila comes to know about the pain and suffering of her dead mother-in-law Mira through her poems and diaries. The protagonist points out that there may be so many women like Akka who are not able to articulate their suffering.

Women are also subjected to rape outside marriage. The novelist, through her women characters, exposes the harsh realities that women have been subjected to in the world of masculine domination. Men have been inflicting sexual violence on women for ages to assert their manhood and supremacy. In Anita Desai's novel, *Fire on the Mountain,*[12] the novelist shows how men like Preet Singh raped and murdered Ila, a social activist, as a revenge for hindering his way to marry his daughter off. Such sexual violence is "the product of a patriarchal evil in which men control both social institutions and women's bodies."[13] Kate Millett rightly observes in *Sexual Politics*:

> Patriarchal societies typically link feelings of cruelty with sexuality, the latter often equated with evil and with power. . . . The rule here associates sadism with the male ("the masculine role") and victimization with the female ("the feminine role"). Emotional response to violence against women in patriarchy is often curiously ambivalent; references to wife-beating for example, invariably produce laughter and some embarrassment.[14]

In *The Binding Vine*, Kalpana had refused to be the second wife to her uncle. To take revenge on her, he had raped her and injured her. She was in coma, fighting for her life. Urmila, the protagonist of the novel, and Bhaskar, the doctor who had examined Kalpana, wanted to record it as a rape case, but Shakutai, the mother of the victim and the police officer who had to handle the case, wanted to record it as an accident for different reasons. The police wanted to do so just to avoid further complication generally associated with the case of rape. His motive was quite different from that of Shakutai. She was really worried about the possible scandal that would follow and its consequences in the future life of her two daughters. She pleaded with Urmi not to tell anyone:

> don't tell anyone, I'll never be able to hold up my head again, who'll marry the girl, we're decent people. If a girl's honour is lost, what's left? The girl doesn't have to do anything wrong, people will always point a finger at her. . . . I have another daughter, what will become of her? (58-59)

Here, it seems that Shakutai was reflecting the attitude of the society that gives too much importance to the institution of marriage and chastity of women. It is quite ironical that the same society has apparently no objection if a man loses his chastity. As Simone de Beauvoir states, "Virginity is valued so highly in many circles that to lose it outside legitimate marriage seems a real disaster. The young girl who yields through impulse or surprise thinks she is dishonoured."[15]

As a mother living in such a society, Shakutai was fully concerned with their place in the society and hence could not think of anything else but to avoid scandal. It was not that she did not want justice, she wanted to share the attitude of the society, but, at the same time she feared its dire consequences upon the future of her family. To her, everything, including justice, was secondary when it came to the question of saving their images in the society. She had three children, two daughters and one son among whom Kalpana was the eldest. From the above-quoted lines, we come to know that Shakutai was worried about her another daughter and her marriage prospect but it seems that she was not at all worried about her son's marriage. Here also, society seems to relax its harshness on males and lets them escape it. When a man rapes a woman outside marriage, his reputation is not so much affected as that of the woman who is the victim.

In our society, women are treated as nothing but merely sexual objects. Man sees woman's body as sex, and in the male psychology a woman's body is a territory to be conquered. And rape is again a means to exploit and silence woman so that she is kept outside communication in male-dominated society. It is ironical that it is the victims but not the culprits who are considered defamed and, even they are condemned, sometimes punished and looked down upon, without any fault of theirs. As mentioned earlier, in extreme cases, in Muslim community, even today, rape victims are killed to save the reputation of the families in the name of "honour killing." Such double standard moral codes aggravate the suffering and victimization of women. This biased treatment of women by the patriarchal society is what the novelist tries to expose.

One of the important aspects of marriage that affects the lives of most women is to give up their hopes and aspirations as soon as they get married. It is mainly because, as Meenakshi Mukherjee points out, "the fulfillment of one's self, however desirable a goal according to the individualistic ideal of Western society has always been alien to Indian tradition, especially when it is achieved at the cost of duty to the family."[16]

However, such restriction is meant for women only, and not for men, hence, another form of exploitation of women is being operated here. That is why "No man would consent to be a woman, but every man wants women to exist."[17] Bhaskar's mother in *The Binding Vine* loved music and she had been learning it as a girl but soon after her marriage she had to stop. She, then, turned her attention to her children, unable to fulfill her ambition. Savitribai Indorekar in *Small Remedies* received discouragement and unfair criticism from all when she tried to pursue her career in singing, except her father-in-law who, on her request, allowed her to learn it. Vidya in *The Dark Holds No Terrors* who loved theatre with "undesirable passion" (15) had to give up acting and directing as her husband and in-laws disapproved. Likewise, Jaya, the protagonist in *That Long Silence*, lost her vitality to write when her husband confronted her over an article she had written that won a prize in a contest. After this incident, she could never write her mind and hence became a failure. Her husband unreasonably charged her by saying how she could reveal them to the world in that way, thinking that the man and the woman in the story were two of them. All these cases show how a social institution like marriage has turned out to be a barrier in woman's life in a tradition-bound society like India.

In a patriarchal society, woman's role is reduced to the role of an obedient daughter, a dutiful wife, a loving and caring mother only, but in the process she has to sacrifice her individuality. This is true of Jaya, in *That Long Silence* who becomes "almost the stereotype of a woman: nervous, incompetent, needing male help and support" (76) after marriage. Before she was not at all like this; she was courageous, self-independent and fearless. She wondered how and when such a drastic change had started. This change from what she was to what she becomes is a creation of marriage. In spite of her success in writing as "Seeta," a regular column in a newspaper, Jaya, as a writer, was no longer satisfied with her kind of writing. Literally, she had stopped writing her mind and heart because she was "scared of hurting Mohan, scared of jeopardizing the only career" (144) she had, her marriage.

Mira in *The Binding Vine* was not prepared for marriage and was very much interested in her studies and literature when she was married off to the man of her parents' choice. In fact, she was a talented poet. We come to know her talent through her daughter-in-law, Urmila, much after her death. Henceforth, her writing talent died a natural death. It may not be wrong to say that marriage closes the door of self-actualization for most women in a society like India. It is often women who have to sacrifice their aspirations and profession for the sake of the family. Both Iqbal (Devi's lawyer) and his wife, Naseem were equally qualified and they dreamt of practising law but only Iqbal could pursue his career. After one year of their marriage, their first son was born, then her sister died and she had to look after her sister's small daughter also. After that she was busy with her second child. Besides, there were Iqbal's old parents to be taken care of, especially, his paralyzed mother. He reasoned that 'someone has to look after the children, my parents' (85). But the sad reality is that that 'someone' has to be the wife all the time. If there's no strict role-division between man and woman, both of them may go for work by helping each other in domestic sphere too. The worth, hopes and aspirations of many a women in our society remain subdued especially in the lower middle class. However, things are changing as many women of today can afford to have domestic helpers and as a result, they can take up some profession or hobby of their liking, at the same time, giving means of livelihood to the other less fortunate fellow women. Women are expected to contend themselves in feeding others, cooking enormous meals, looking after the children and the old.

In these ways, numerous malpractices defile this institution. Marriage becomes almost a negative term to them. Indu in *Roots and Shadows* says that marriage has given her the "gift of silence" (33) and "an immense capacity for deception" (38). When Hemant, her cousin, tells her that marriage is a trap, she questions herself and gets the answer too:

> A trap? Or a cage? Maybe the comic strip version of the marriage . . . a cage with two trapped animals glaring hatred at each other . . .

> isn't so wrong after all. And it's not a joke, but a tragedy. But what animal would cage itself? (61)

Jaya, in *That Long Silence*, sees herself and her husband as a pair of bullocks yoked together (7). Akka, Indu's grandmother, considered marriage as punishment as she said to Narmada when the latter was getting married: "Now your punishment begins, Narmada. You have to pay for all those saris and jewels" (70). Marriage comes in the way of individual development of women. Whether they are from high or low class, they are subjected to some degree of suppression in one way or the other. Most women characters in the novels of Shashi Deshpande find marriage a bondage that curbs their individuality and, this is true in our society too. If society gives women the stamp of inferiority at the very moment they are born, marriage gives the license to suppress them. However the novelist is not against the institution of marriage but against all those malpractices that defile it. Instead of bringing harmony among people, it is misused as a means to curb freedom and individuality of women.

There are very few women who have dared to cross the barrier set-up by the society in search of their identity. Unlike many other women, Savitribai Indorekar, in *Small Remedies*, in order to pursue her career as a singer, gave up everything, including her marriage and daughter. Music came first in her life, then others follow—her social status and reputation. It was because of her single-minded pursuit that she could become what she wanted, in spite of many barriers. It was not so easy for a woman born and brought up in an orthodox Hindu family and then, married to an upper class family, even to think of learning music, let alone becoming professional. For this, she had to pay a heavy price in the form of lifelong rejection by her own and only daughter, Munni. In addition to this, she had to bear the blame for having walked out of her marriage, her husband and family and eloped with a man, a Muslim with whom she stayed unmarried. Leela, another character from the same novel was an active member of the Communist Party who had been working hard for the party but sidelined while men who had worked under her got the top of the hierarchy. Here, gender discrimination operated. This is a fine example of being "sidelined and marginalized by the patriarchal symbolic order."[18] Later, when she got remarried after becoming a widow, she was disowned by her parents who considered her "the black sheep of the family" (22). However, the same society accepts when a man has a mistress or more than one wife at a time. Shashi Deshpande was successful in exposing such unequal treatment of men and women in a patriarchal society by deliberately presenting and intertwining the stories of Savitribai Indorekar and Ghulaam Saab in the same flow of narration, side by side. While she was looked down upon, his deserted family accepted Ghulaam Saab with open arms. On the other hand, the coming back of Bai to her husband and in-laws was unthinkable. In this context, the novelist, through the mouthpiece of Madhu, seems to be critical of society's different yardsticks adopted for men and women:

> But my father was accepted and his peculiarities and foibles were overlooked, because . . . being a man, he could get away with much. He could live the ways he wanted, without open censure or disapproval. It was not so with Munni's mother. As Savitri Bai Indorekar the singer-woman, some oddities in her behaviour were permitted, possibly tolerated, but it didn't take away the aura of disapproval, or the curiosity, either. (138-39)

Saru, in *The Dark Holds No Terrors* was determined to prove her worth when she felt she was neglected as a child. She joined a medical college much against the wishes of her mother who wanted to get her married off instead. Later she married Manohar, and thus belonged to a different caste, a decision of her own. She became very successful as a doctor and earned more than her husband who worked as lecturer in a third-rate college. She had to undergo many struggles and much suffering for being a disobedient daughter, and for becoming higher in status than her husband and for proving her individuality. Kalpana in *The Binding Vine,* who was independent and fearless both in thought and action, was subjected to brutal rape; she remained in coma for days in hospital. In patriarchal set-up, there is less scope of proving a woman's worth and even her desire to excel is not approved of. They have to forget themselves as individuals and devote themselves to the traditionally accepted role. Only then, they will be accepted and appreciated by the society. If, on the other hand, they dare defy the rigid norms and customs of the society, they have to bear the brunt all through their lives.

But women belonging to the lower or middle class are often made scapegoats. In spite of their sincere efforts and hard work to earn for the family and to maintain their home and children, women are frequently blamed. It is ironical that even children blame their mothers but not their fathers even when the latter fail to be responsible. What Mandira told Urmila about her mother in *The Binding Vine* is obvious. She blamed her mother only but not her father—both working—for leaving them alone:

> 'You know, Urmi aunti, when I grow up, I'm never going to leave my children to go to work.'
>
> 'What will you do?'
>
> 'Stay at home and look after them.'
>
> 'When they grow up, they'll go away and won't need you. What will you do then?'
>
> 'Then I'll go and work.'
>
> 'Who'll give you a job when you're that old?'
>
> 'I don't care; I'll never leave my children alone. (72)

This is not the voice of Mandira but of the society that has strict role-division between males and females, much to the advantage of the former. Here, Deshpande seems to question such unequal treatment when Vanaa asked Urmila why nobody thought of blaming her husband even though he was never around. The expectation of the society that women only should take care of the children and do the household chores is still prevalent in all sections of Indian society. It is because people still believe in the age-old view: "Man exists in the social world. For the women, however her place is within home."[19] In the lower class, we have the case of Kalpana blaming her mother when her father left her mother for another woman. Kalpana's father was a drunkard, a good-for-nothing fellow and very irresponsible. On the contrary, her mother, Shakutai was one of those numerous women of her class who worked really hard to make both ends meet single-handedly. She had done all kinds of work without any complaint. She even looked after a paralytic old woman for a year, cleaning up her filth. She did it all so that her children could grow up, go to school and live better than her. In spite of her hard work and sacrifices, her children blamed her but not her husband who spent all his time and money on drinking and gambling. Jaya in *That Long Silence*, in her early days of married life, asked Mohan, her husband, to cook the food that day to which he only smiled, thinking that she was just joking. She connected this incident to one such in her childhood days when she stayed in her grandfather's house. She heard her cousin, Sujata, ask her aunties when she was told to do some clearing up:

> 'Then why can't the boys do it? Jaanu or Shridhar? Why does it have to be me and Veena?' They had all laughed at that, genuine amused laughter, Sujata herself too, and even Ajji had smiled her small, rare smile. (81)

Their "genuine amused laughter" indicates that they did not take the thing seriously. It is because they are born and brought up in a society where the roles of men and women are divided into water-tight compartments. Such role divisions might have served some purpose when men used to go for hunting, and women remain at home, bearing and rearing children, doing household chores and kitchen gardening. That was in the pre-historic age, but now we are in the modern age where men and women are educated and trained in various fields to prove their excellence. They both go out for work and it seems to be an injustice to expect the same age-old roles when almost everything has changed. Such rigid roles seem to be of less necessity. Earlier, it might serve the purposes of both men and women but now it serves only the interest of men, much to the disadvantage of women. It is high time for both men and women to look into these problems and understand the need to rectify age-old norms. And the sooner, the better; or else as long as the imbalance persists, the unhappy situation will remain unchanged in the society.

ii) Problems faced by educated modern Indian women

Educated modern Indian women face the dilemma between conforming to the traditional beliefs and following the modern outlook acquired from their education. Nazneen Khan observes:

> Shashi Deshpande is well acquainted with the dilemma of the modern, educated middle class Indian woman who has to continue to play the role of the propagator of human race and housewife on the one hand and that also that of a human being with a vocation, seeking full expression of her personality on the other hand.[20]

They suffer in both the cases. They have to suffer mentally when they are confined to tradition against their wishes. They have to suffer if they choose the other way too. Sarita, in *The Dark Holds No Terrors* observes, "It was so much easier for women in those days to accept, not to struggle, because they believed, they knew there was nothing else for them. And they called that Fate" (70). Traditional women like Saru's grandmother could submit to her fate much easier than her younger counterparts. As a married woman, Kalyani had suffered enough for 35 long years in *A Matter Of Time* and she easily gave up everything to fate when she witnessed her daughter Sumi's marriage broken as the latter's husband had walked out. Jaya in *That Long Silence* could not help but envy her maidservant, Jeeja, who never complained about her suffering. She endured with silence as if enduring was a part of life. There seemed to be no anger behind that silence. Modern-educated women like Saru, Jaya and Sumi wished if they could also submit all the burdens and sufferings to the unknown and mysterious 'Fate.' They feel helpless in most cases as they are bound to the strict rules set by tradition while their modern, educated minds tell just the contrary.

In most societies, women and passion are alien to each other, which in actuality is not true. Society expects them to be shy, submissive and dependent on men. These are the views repeatedly reflected in most films and fiction. Contrary to such views, Deshpande presents, in her novels, women who are modern in their outlook, who consider sex as a physical need rather than as a taboo. She explores this aspect by presenting women having passion against the traditional belief that they lack and suffer from lack of orgasm: "I become in an instant a physically aroused woman, with an infinite capacity for loving and giving, with a passionate desire to be absorbed by the man I loved'' (40). Generally, it seems that men have difficulty to accept passion in women.

Women of all classes face the problem of expressing their passion, desire and sexuality. They are looked down upon as unwomanly if they express it. It is true in the field of literature too where women writers have to think twice before they write about female sexuality. Virginia Woolf rightly observes regarding the predicament of women writers:

> she had thought of something, something about the body, about the passions which it was unfitting for her as a woman to say. Men, her reason told her, would be shocked. The consciousness of what men will say of a woman who speaks the truth about her passions had roused her from her artist's state of unconsciousness.[21]

This is true of all women in a male-dominated society.

Men have a high regard for chastity in women though most of them do not consider the same for themselves. In *Small Remedies,* the marriage of Som and Madhu began to deteriorate when she narrated much later, one of her childhood incidents. She told him that she had slept with one of her father's friends in his attempt to console her when the bad news of her father's death was announced. She also confessed that it was not rape and she had been a willing participant in it. This incident affected their marriage so much. Madhu recalled their first night when she saw a look of puzzle and then of regret on Som's face when she encouraged him by saying it was all right and she wanted it too. In *Roots and Shadows,* Indu was quite surprised and shocked when Jayant, her husband, who was "so passionate, so ready" (83) refused when she took the initiative.

> When I'm like that, he turns away from me. I've learnt my lesson now. And so I pretend. I'm passive and unresponsive. I'm still and dead. And now I know . . . it shocks him to find passion in a woman. It puts him off. (83)

It is, perhaps, considered unwomanly when a woman expresses her passion. Ironically, even when a woman is raped against her wish, she is considered unchaste and unclean. So, in both the cases, it is woman who is made a victim. Women like Jiji in *Moving On* and Devi in *In the Country of Deceit* are called cheap and low when they have physical relationship outside and without marriage. It's always women on whom the society puts the burden of guarding the social and moral codes strictly, while letting men have their own ways and freedom regarding the same.

Women are upset whenever they face any unequal treatment between men and women in the patriarchal society. As mentioned earlier, Jaya in *That Long Silence*, questioned herself why not a single woman's name was there in the long two hundred years old family tree. The matter was so disturbing that she neither could overlook the injustice done to women nor did she ignore it; but she dared not ask any question openly to her 'Ramukaka' regarding the matter. This inner conflict makes their lives miserable. Their real sorrow lies when social conditions and traditional beliefs bind them in spite of their modern outlook. Sometimes, such outlook and their intelligence seem to work against them as reflected in *Roots and Shadows* when the old uncle of Indu told her that intelligence was always a burden for a woman.

Educated women are well aware of their place in the patriarchal society and hence, they cannot freely exercise their independent mind and spirit. They are often frustrated as they seem to see wide difference between what they had been taught and trained in a traditional society and the modern outlook they acquire from their education. What Indira Nityanandam states in this regard may be noted: "Indian women face a painful choice whether to use their mind and education as they deem fit or to surrender themselves to the new family they enter with marriage."[22]
Nevertheless, some of them are able to come out of their helpless situation, and ready to face problems of all kinds as they gain self-confidence after enduring much pain and suffering.

iii) Problems faced by lower class women

Lower class women are mostly illiterate and traditional in their outlook. They have to take on all the responsibilities and bear burden of their family—bringing up their children, maintaining and marrying off their daughters, as their husbands are irresponsible and drunkards. They, unlike those educated, modern, working women, can easily submit all their sufferings and misfortunes to their fate. They hardly question the existing system even when it works against them. These women suffer more than those belonging to the higher class. In *The Binding Vine,* Shakutai wanted the rape case to be registered as an accident to avoid scandal, which would definitely affect the marriage prospect of her two daughters. On the other hand, Urmila wanted to fight against such injustice by filing it as a rape case and punish the culprit. The victim was still in coma, lying unconscious in the hospital while the culprit was set free. Educated, modern, independent women like Urmila may easily overlook such things but for an uneducated woman like Shakutai, such small things are the basis of their life.

Having been born a woman means to accept shackles much to the disadvantage of the woman, but then being born in the lower class might mean to have double disadvantage for women. They are generally neglected by our society. If the new feminism is a matter of choice, then these underprivileged women, with all their limitations and no educational background, have practically no other choice than drudgery as rightly pointed out by Rashmi Gaur that "the drudgery and work does not liberate such women, it only reminds them of their economic and class oppression. Work does not constitute a choice in their life."[23] Even for a small thing, they have to depend on others. Shakutai needed an Urmila to draw the medical attention to her daughter. Women like Jeeja, in *That Long Silence*, needed a Jaya to make the doctor look after her son better. She requested Jaya, "If you speak to the doctor there, they will look after him better; they will give him special care. Otherwise no one cares, no one is bothered about poor patients, they won't even tell us anything if we ask them, they bark at us as if we're dogs." (160)

The importance of marriage for such a class of women is not exaggerated though. Bhaskar in *The Binding Vine* asked out of curiosity if getting married was so important to a woman. Urmila replied in positive, saying that it was so important for women of this class for it protects women from other men. Bhaskar still wondered why Shakutai worried so much for her daughter's marriage when she herself had nothing out of marriage, except children and an irresponsible husband. In *That Long Silence*, Jeeja sternly shut up her step daughter-in-law, Tara, when the latter wished her drunkard husband dead. Jeeja herself had enough of her suffering but still she attached much value and importance to wifehood. She said to Tara, "Don't forget, he keeps the kumkum on your forehead. What is a woman without that?" (53) In *A Matter of Time*, Sumi wondered to see her mother enjoy and celebrate her wifehood, applying 'kumkum' and moving in the company of women with the pride of a wife, in spite of the fact that her husband had stopped living and communicating with her for 35 years. Sumi recalled one old woman advising her to go back to her husband, saying that woman is nothing without her husband.

It is apparent that most of these women suffer because they attach too much to the value of wifehood and motherhood. Sulu, Shakutai's younger sister, had an unsuccessful marriage just because she was childless. She lived with constant fear if her husband would throw her out and took another wife. He developed a kind of liking for her sister's daughter, Kalpana. So, he threatened her if she failed to give Kalpana to him, he would throw her out of the house. She was not the only one who suffered this lot. Jeeja, in *That Long Silence*, too had suffered silently when her husband left her to marry another woman. She expressed her sufferings to Jaya, "How could I blame him for marrying again when I couldn't give him any children? How could I blame that woman for marrying him? With whom shall I be angry?" (52) It seems the society considers women to be worthless if she can not become a mother. However, such a notion is rarely found in the middle-class educated women of our society. Indu in *Roots and Shadows* firmly declared that she would not have any child that would not be wholly welcome. Self-assertion is what women like Indu have, but among the uneducated women it is non-existent.

iv) Individual problems faced by women

Under this sub-heading, individual problems faced by women are studied. Shashi Deshpande, as a novelist, is not in favour of the politicizing of women's problems and generalization of the same. In the novel, *The Dark Holds No Terrors*, there is an interesting chapter about the meeting after a long time of the old three friends—Nalu, Saru and Smita. Through their conversation, we come to know that they are three different persons with different attitudes. What Deshpande emphasizes is that they are women no doubt, but that does not necessarily mean that they have similar points of view nor do they have the same problems. Women's problems are as separate and varied as they are different individuals. Smita is a fun-loving, easy-going and financially, physically and emotionally a dependent person whose life is centred on her husband only. She is happy and satisfied with her life being a wife and mother of three outwardly to a limited extent, and deep down she is not so happy as she is a dependent on her husband financially. One can see her meagre existence with financial difficulties when her husband has that scissor-cutting method of giving her money irrespective of her need to meet the social demands. She implores Saru to lend her just one hundred rupees with which she would be able to buy a sari for her sister-in-law whose son would have his thread ceremony. Her insensitive husband has no understanding of this and he gives money enough to buy a small gift for the boy. It is pathetic to see the way she plans to give back the money to Saru—by saving some small portion of the money to be given by her husband every time. The whole thing speaks of the delicate situations a woman faces, when she lives at the mercy of a stingy husband without economic freedom. And here Deshpande is at her best to extricate this kind of women's lives, a typical example of Indian woman at home facing martyrdom everyday. In this connection what Saru thinks is right:

> Nalu would say that it was marriage and men that had degraded Smita. But Smita had done it even in those days lying at home about where she went and what she did, getting money from her mother for books and splashing it in the canteen. So perhaps, it was really Smita after all. (119)

Other women on the contrary are quite different. Nalu is a spinster who is serious and dedicated to her job. Saru, the protagonist, is one who manages both her career and family. Smita does not mind changing her name to 'Geetanjali' or 'Anju' after marriage as per her husband's wish. But Nalu takes a strong exception to this for it amounts to losing one's identity—female self-identity and she insists on her calling her as Smita still and not by any other name.

Deshpande does not believe in generalizing women's problems, as pointed out before. Smita's problems are Smita's own. Saru's marital problems are partly a creation of her own. It's true that any man would feel uncomfortable to have a wife far more successful than himself, considering the kind of society we have, and hence reflection of it in their relationship is quite possible. In the novel, Manohar does the same—trying to assert his manhood by inflicting pain and raping his wife, and such cases are quite common in our society. However, the prolonging of this problem seems to arise out of their own personal behaviour. For instance, Saru, instead of facing and understanding the problem, turns a blind eye to it, pretending that it's just a nightmare. She was too occupied and eager to absorb all the attention and respect her new profession showers upon her to notice the boredom, hurt and neglected look of her husband. Her problem at home—the brutal and jealous vengeance of her not quite successful husband for becoming a successful doctor is partly Saru's own. Nalu's unhappiness and bitterness, despite she being a spinster, are none else's but her own. What is important is that the novelist in these matters sees things not belonging to women as a class but to women as individuals. She does not generalize but particularizes. So her feminist ideology is not guided by a common bond of women as such.

Thus women's problems of different proportions have been highlighted in the different light and shade in Deshpande's novels. Mother-daughter hatred can be seen in the case of Saru and her mother who almost disowns her daughter whom she thinks responsible for the death of her only son. Later, Saru's marriage to Manohar, a man of her choice, turns out to be sour when she becomes professionally more successful as a doctor than her husband who was just a mere teacher in a college. This leads to her sexual harassment by her husband. But all this is not women's problem, but of an individual woman's problem.

Deshpande in *A Matter of Time* provides an account of husband-wife tussle that affects children. Gopal left his family for reasons not known to him very clearly and that had an adverse effect on the life of his wife Sumi and their daughters. While Sumi suffered silently and stoically, her teenage daughters tried every means to bring their parents together. When all her attempts failed, Aru, the eldest daughter, sought help and advice from Surekha, a woman activist and lawyer, to demand maintenance from their father. Thus one problem leads to another. Her mother was much worried about the whole situation in which Aru was trapped. Sumi speaks to Gopal:

> But I don't think she's good for Aru at this time. Making what has happened in our family part of the war between men and women—no I don't like that. (220)

These are individual problems, not classified as general. Some such cases are in other novels of Deshpande. Deshpande herself says in an interview, "each person is an individual in a novel and you can't apply any general principles to them."[24]

Lastly, it may be observed that women of all classes suffer not because they lack something but mostly because of the culturally construct roles that are assigned to them by the patriarchal system. It is high time to understand that:

> Woman is not an essence but a construct in the domain of patriarchal culture, a dispersed subject, historically variable, socially feminised and a site on which masculine meanings get spoken and masculine desire enacted.[25]

Most women of Shashi Deshpande struggle in silence for a very long time but a few of them are able to come to terms with their problems. They find a kind of balance, harmony and meaning in life as they are no longer confused with themselves. Their approach is neither total acceptance nor rejection. It is a kind of the mixture of the two in the sense that they accept and acknowledge the value of family and the need to live within relationships and society but reject those oppressive systems and values patriarchy nurtures for the suppression of women. The stage of acceptance and rejection is Deshpande's concept of women's growth and enlightenment.

NOTES

1. Simone De Beauvoir, "Introduction," *The Second Sex*, xxii.
2. *Ibid.*, 267.
3. Mukta Gupta, "Girl Child: A Neglected Dimension," *Issues Related to Women* (New Delhi: Sarup, 2000), 99.
4. Kamala Das, "An Introduction," Vinayak Krishna Gokak, ed., *The Golden Treasury of Indo-Anglian Poetry (1828-1965)* (Delhi: Pencraft, 1998), 272-73.
5. Kalindi Muzumdar, "Women and Violence: A Human Rights Perspective," Shirin K. and Sabiha Al-Issa, ed., *Violence against Women: Women against Violence* (Delhi: Pencraft, 1998), 39.
6. K. Nirupa Rani, "Woman, Society and Religion: Tehmina Durrani's Quest for Identity" *The Literary Criterion*, Vol. XXXVIII, No. 3 and 4 (2003): 45.
7. Virginia Woolf, *A Room of One's Own*, 44.
8. Geetha Gangadharan, "Denying the Otherness" (Interview), R.S. Pathak, ed., *The Fiction of Shashi Deshpande*, 253.
9. Qtd. Mallladi Subbamma, "Mother Teresa's Utterances," trans. M.V. Ramamurthy, *Women, Tradition and Culture*, 102.
10. *Ibid.*, 103.
11. Kate Millett, *Sexual Politics* (Rpt. London: Virago, 1977), 144.
12. Anita Desai, *Fire on the Mountain* (London: Vintage, 1999).
13. Maggie Humm, *The Dictionary of Feminist Theory* (Rpt. London: Harvester Wheatsheaf, 1995), 293.
14. Kate Millett, *Sexual Politics*, 44-45.
15. Simone de Beauvoir, *The Second Sex*, 380.
16. Cited K. Meera Bai, "The Conformists" *Women's Voices; The Novels of Indian Writers* (New Delhi: Prestige, 1960), 63.
17. Simone de Beauvoir, *The Second Sex*, 141.
18. Toril Moi, "Feminist Literary Criticism," Ann Jafferson and David Robey, ed., *Modern Literary Theory* (London: B.T. Batsford 1986), 212.
19. Anne Foreman, "Feminity as Alienation: Women and the Family" *Marxism and Psychoanalysis* (London: Pluto, 1977), 10.
20. Nazneen Khan, "Woman 'Made' Woman in the Novels of Shashi Deshpande" *Pegasus—A Journal of Literary and Critical Studies*. Vol. IV, Jan.-Dec. (2005), 57.
21. Virginia Woolf, "'Professions for Women' The Death of the Moth," Mary Eagleton, ed., *Feminist Literary Theory: A Reader*, 78-80.

22. Indira Nityanandam, "Assimilation or Alienation: A Study of Monisha in Anita Desai's *Voices in the City* and Geeta in Rama Mehta's *Inside the Haveli*," R.K. Dhawan, ed., *Indian Women Novelists*. Set II, Vol. 1 (New Delhi: Prestige, 1993), 72.
23. Rashmi Gaur, "Images of Indian Women in Shashi Deshpande's *That Long Silence*: Stereotypes, Myths and Realities," *Women's Writing: Some Facets*, 74.
24. S. Prasanna Sree, "An Interview with Shashi Deshpande," Amarnath Prasad, ed., *New Lights on Indian Women Novelists in English*, 94.
25. K.K. Ruthven, *Feminist Literary Studies: An Introduction* (London: Cambridge, 1984), 45.

Women's Liberation vis-à-vis Economic Liberation

The importance of economic independence to improve the lot, status and position of women is generally felt by most feminists, both at home and abroad. Western feminists since Elizabeth Cady Stanton, Simone de Beauvoir and Virginia Woolf lay emphasis on having women's own income to free themselves from the dependency syndrome. Women's liberation and economic independence are related issues. Elizabeth Cady Stanton wrote: "When women can support themselves, have their entry to all the trades and professions, with a house of their own over their heads and a bank account, they will own their bodies and be dictators in the social realm."[1]

Virginia Woolf in her books, especially *A Room of One's Own* and *Three Guineas*,[2] emphasizes women's need to earn an income of their own by entering into some professions. Woolf stresses the link between economic independence and individual identity of a woman. In fact, financial independence is often regarded as almost synonymous with women's emancipation in most Western countries where there is less constraint of culture, tradition and customs. However, a close study reveals that such is not always the case in India. It is generally assumed that if a woman is earning, she can do anything with her money, but sadly, in our country, various factors like culture, social norms and etiquettes come in the way. Therefore, in India, economic liberation of women may work positively, at the same time, negatively towards women's liberation.

Shashi Deshpande feels and experiences the need and importance of financial and material conditions like Virginia Woolf as she remarks in an interview. Whatever the case may be, a woman needs money to sustain her life and profession if any. Virginia Woolf speaks of the importance of material conditions in which one works. As she says, 'Dogs will bark, people will interrupt, money has to be made.' This is true at any time in one's life.[3]

Like their creator, most heroines of Shashi Deshpande feel the need to earn an income of their own. In *Roots and Shadows*, Indu works as a journalist for a reputed women magazine that earns her a fair amount of money. Saru in *The Dark Holds No Terrors* works hard and becomes a successful doctor. From the very beginning, when she was a small kid, she realized the importance of financial independence after she had heard the story of her grandmother, who, after being deserted by her husband, came back to her father.

After the initial charm of the newly married life had died down, she and her husband were exposed to reality and, consciousness of the need to earn money was all the more felt. She realized, "I knew now that without money life became petty and dreary. The thought of going on in this way became unbearable" (92). Her husband tried to make both ends meet with his meagre income as a lecturer in some third-rate college. He took tuitions, "Trying to get English into the thick heads of the boys with rich fathers" (157). He had forgotten to celebrate the joy of becoming a father as the financial burden was so heavy. He said, "I had imagined that to have a child of your own would be one of the life's greatest experiences. Now I can only think of the price of baby food and baby powders" (157). To live without any income but with such a husband, any woman's sad predicament would not be an exaggeration. Most women in India who do not earn suffer the wrath and whims of many a worse husband.

In *That long Silence,* though Jaya does not have any well defined career, she does not sit idle doing household chores only. She is a columnist and aspiring fiction writer. Her regular column called "Seeta" earns her both fame and money. The need to have one's income is not necessarily confined to this elite class of women only but also to women of lower class who do not have the opportunity to learn and educate themselves. Her maid servant, Jeeja earns money and maintains her family when her husband gets remarried to another woman as she is barren. She is a thorough professional and has dignity of labour. She feels proud of her work and manages to earn more than the other maids because of her "reputation of reliability" (51). Shakutai, Kalpana's mother, in *The Binding Vine*, is another unfortunate woman left by her drunkard husband for another woman. She, like Jeeja, maintains her family by earning her own money as a maid servant. Urmi, the protagonist, is also a woman who wants to rely on herself financially and otherwise too. Though her husband Kishore, who is in merchant navy and lives away from her most of the time, sends her money regularly, Urmi insists on using her own money as far as possible. When Vaana, her childhood friend and sister-in-law asked her why she does not want to use her husband's money, Urmi ruminates, "she does not understand that I intend to live on my own money I earn, that I will use Kishore's money only when I have to" (94).

Sumi is one who does not compromise as an individual. She neither interferes with others' decision and individual space, not even with her husband's decision to leave her and family life for good, nor does she let others interfere with her in any way. She bears all the sufferings and uncertainties of life stoically and still maintains her individual self and independence. When her husband Gopal has left her, she has to come back and stay in her parental home, along with her three grown up daughters. It is such a "Big House" (123) that would comfortably accommodate all of them. However, Sumi begins searching for a rented house as she does not want to be a burden on anybody. She reacts to her own parents, "I have no right to be here . . . I feel like a parasite" (71). Many people like Gopal's nephew, her own father and sister, and Ramesh—offer her the much needed financial help at her hour of need when she badly needs money to maintain her family, buy books and clothes for the girls and pay their fees besides other things they need, she does not take it, entirely depending on her own money. Money is very important in life, but that is not the only important one for many women characters in Deshpande's novels; the question of individual dignity comes first.

Madhu in *Small Remedies* becomes financially independent from a young age. She was brought up single-handedly by her father who was a doctor. Before his death, he handed her over to her maternal aunt Leela, when she was only fifteen years. After some years the money her father had left for her was exhausted. She is not ready to take anybody's help. Even her uncle Joe is ready to support her studies but, sensing her desire to support herself, he offers money saying, "look upon it as a loan . . . pay me back when you start earning" (83). Madhu is determined, "I will start working, I will earn my own money, become independent" (83). By then as if it is a godsend she is offered a job in a magazine *City Views*. Her uncle, Joe, is not happy but her aunt, being an independent woman herself and also knowing the value and importance of earning one's own money, is reconciled. Madhu, on her part, enjoys with her new-found freedom and space given by her job and money. She seems to be on cloud nine when she says, "I have everything I want: work I enjoy, an income of my own, room to live in" (85). She now, no longer lives with her uncle and aunt and does not take Maruti Chawl home offered by her aunt because she wants something she can call her own. That 'something' to her seems to be as she says:

> A tiny bathroom, the size of a toilet in trains and another little space in the corridor which becomes my kitchen, complete my new home. To me it's heaven. Lying on my narrow bed on the divan in my almost bare cell like room, I have a sense of absolute freedom, of soaring in space. Even the monsoon beaten grey dingy walls of the next building, the only view I have from my window, can't quench my joy, my sense of having grown wings. I am happier than I have been for years (85-86).

As mentioned earlier, Leela, her aunt, "was an unusual woman, ahead not only of her generation, but the next one as well" (94). She always supported herself. When her first husband died, she took up a job instead of sitting and complaining about her fate. She helped her family and educated her brother-in-law. Even after getting remarried to Joe, "a doctor with a fairly good income, she continued to live on her own money." (94). Lata, a minor character who was a distant relative to Madhu, felt that she had to do her job, bearing the burden and responsibility of maintaining her family equally with her husband as she confided to Madhu, "but I can't give up my job, we need the money" (94). In the same novel, Savitribai Indorekar is also an example of an independent woman who earned both fame and money as a singer despite being born and brought up and married to a traditional, orthodox Hindu family. In the novel, *Moving On,* Jiji feels the need to earn to maintain herself and her kids after her husband's death, and chooses not to be a dependent on her parents. She works as an 'ayah in a school, salesgirl, typist, P.T. teacher, nurse almost to an old man' (215). In the latest novel, Devayani or Devi has taken up many small jobs like taking tuition, supervising the household works of Kshama to keep her busy and to earn money too. Kusuma, her domestic help, walks out of her broken marriage without having a second thought because she knows her worth as an excellent cook and she can earn enough money to support herself. Talking about the divorce case of an American couple, Sindhu comments that the law of the land is good enough to grant the wife the fifty percent of their property and opines: 'we should have such a law at home, so that women don't become homeless beggars the moment their marriage is over' (160).

Deshpande's women characters belong to both middle and lower classes striving to support themselves financially. In most cases it does improve their condition, position and status in and outside the family. Some of them are able to find happiness and job satisfaction as well. However, the other side of the story is that financial independence does not guarantee women's emancipation; rather, it works against the welfare of women in cases where they earn more than their husbands as it happens to Saru and her husband. This is because patriarchal society favours male supremacy, and in such situations women's financial independence makes a man more hostile and brutal towards women. It is because a man thinks he is superior to his wife in every respect, and if his wife earns more than what he does his sexist attitude is more obvious. In this regard, N. Sharada Iyer says: "Even economically independent women have not been able to clear off the besetting pitfalls created by the customs and beliefs sedulously preserved in the tradition bound Indian society."[4]

All this means that women's financial power and economic independence do not and cannot downplay the traditional gender bias against women. Even in societies where matrilineal structure, prevails women have become second class citizens, not able to come to the centre when important matters are discussed. This can be seen in the khasi community in Meghalaya, where women do not change their condition and status even if they are in better financial position. Women of this community enjoy special privilege of inheriting and owning parental properties but still they are not allowed to take part in family discussions as happened in some other similar communities like that of Kamala Das. She belongs to a matrilineal society where women are generally economically empowered. But decision making rests with man only, and the lives of the matriarchs "were nothing more than 'events in the destiny of men.'"[5]

Akka in *Roots and Shadows* reminds us of such a fate. Although Akka was respected by all her brothers, she was excluded from the family discussions. Akka was financially independent besides being the authority of the family. But her authority ceases to exist when important decision-making meetings are held—she is excluded, and her presence is almost reduced to zero. Similarly, Indu's educational and economic position had no value to the traditional mindset of her family. To them, she was nothing more than a childless woman.

Deshpande brings out another seamy side of women's economic independence. Economic independence is often bound with compromise. Sometimes money, instead of helping a person to be independent, becomes an obstacle in his/her attempt to attain self-independence. For example, Indu does not enjoy the kind of work she is doing. One can see her fate; she is a woman of character, straight, honest, and being a journalist of a popular women's magazine she is uncompromising. But to be uncompromising and to be economically independent are opposed to each other specially in view of the present hypocritical world, where honesty counts less but flattery counts more. Her own experience by compeering two versions of a woman, one by herself and another by an old man, whose views are ruthlessly "of a shameless" exploitative woman, blind to any moral concern "in pursuit of fame, power and money" (16) as against her version of the woman as a "soft-spoken, articulate, seemingly sincere and dedicated," and acceptance of her version by the editor despite the irreversible fact of the old man's version is a rude shock to her. She knows the editor, for his survival, has to accept her eulogy. Indeed, for money and for survival, one needs to make compromises, and to intend to resign on principle is foolish as Indu's husband reacts to her:

> That's life! What can one person do against the whole system! No point making yourself ridiculous with futile gesture. We need the money, don't we? Don't forget, we have a long way to go. (17)

Thus, Indu has to go on for a long time doing the same monotonous job that appeals neither to her interest nor her conscience just because of money.

Another negative aspect of women's economic independence arises when the wife earns more than the husband as encountered by Saru in *The Dark Holds No Terrors*. In a patriarchal society like India, if the husband earns more or becomes the only earning member of the family, happiness and peace prevail in the family. The same case is not there if the wife happens to earn more than the husband as it is against the scale of tradition. This makes Saru express "a+b they told us in mathematics is equal to b+a. But a+b was not, definitely equal to b+a" (42). This statement holds true to Indian society where man and superiority seem to be almost synonymous. As observed by S. Anandlakshmi: "The supremacy of the male is so well established that the average Indian is surprised to even be queried about it. Whatever the ecology of the social group, even in communities where the women may be the bread-winner, the male is considered superior."[6]

It is the financial imbalance of the husband and the wife in the socio-cultural context of India that often disturbs the once happily married life. Tony and Cynthia in *If I Die Today* were happy with each other before their marriage and the fact that Cynthia is a doctor who earns more than Tony who is a Games master begins to matter much just after marriage all of a sudden. Cynthia feels that Tony is suffering from inferiority complex and "his going down hill" may be associated with her being a doctor. She thinks, "If I'd given up my job and become the pathetically clinging female, may be things could have gone right between us." (95)

Financial factor plays a very important role in the power politics of man-woman relationship. This is so in *The Dark Holds No Terrors*. When his wife Saru earns more and when she becomes very popular, the manhood and self confidence of Manohar undergo a drastic change rendering him impotent for the first time in their married life. Their relationship was even more badly affected when she had been helped by her teacher Boozie by giving her a hefty loan to boost her profession which leads to her opening of consulting rooms. She was less angry with the people around when they all glared at her and Boozie when the latter put his hands on her shoulder nor was with Boozie who did that just to show his virility and masculinity by masquerading his being a gay than with her husband, who remained quite unconcerned with the financial involvement. Financial disparity between the husband and wife, the husband's low earning and the wife's better financial position seriously keep the husband-wife relationship off the balance. Saru and her husband are examples of this.

Money power is something that undermines the ego of man, and to compensate for the loss of that, man turns to vengeful animal brutishness. In this connection, two incidents may be cited. One was when a girl who came to interview Saru casually asked Manu how he felt when his wife earned more than him. His anger was expressed when he behaved like an animal hurting Saru that night as she said, "He attacked me like an animal that night; I was sleeping and I woke up and there was this . . . this man hurting me. With his hands, his teeth, his whole body" (201). The second incident that further exacerbated their already deteriorated marital life was when they met one of his friends and his wife on their way to Ooty:

> 'Going somewhere?' The man asked, looking down at the suitcase.
>
> 'Yes, we're having a small holiday.'
>
> 'Where?'
>
> 'Down South. Ooty for a few days, Bangalore and Mysore on the way.' . . .

> 'Lucky fellow. We've been dreaming of Matheran for years. Can't afford even that.'
>
> 'If you had married a doctor,' the wife said tartly, 'you'd have gone to Ooty too.' (111)

The same night, she received, "the monstrous assault" with "hurting hands and the savage teeth" (112). Saru being tired of everything, especially the unhappy situation they're in, told her husband that she wanted to stop working but her husband reasoned her, like Indu's husband did in *Roots and Shadows*:

> 'And how will we live?' . . .
>
> 'On my salary? Come on, Saru, don't be silly. You know how much I earn. You think we can live this way on that? . . . Can you bear to send the children to a third-rate school? To buy them the cheapest clothes, the cheapest of everything? To save and scrape and still have nothing after the first few days of the month? No, Saru, there can be no going back. We have to go on' (81)

Saru was now in a fix. Her financial independence was of no use to her. "The very economic independence, on the strength of which she had become independent, now becomes her bane."[7] Her belief "that economic independence alone could be an insurance against subordination or suppression"[8] became a shattering fantasy. She and her husband were happy as long as they depended on the meagre income of her husband amidst all the hardships and inconveniences. Saru said:

> It was heaven, in spite of the corridors smelling of urine, the rooms with their dank scaled-in odours, women with inquisitive, unfriendly eyes, men with lascivious stares. And we were happy. (40)

Deshpande makes it clear that patriarchal society does not encourage women to be independent and if women become more efficient, competent and do better than their husbands, the society tries every means to thwart them, suppress them. As Saru says:

> Don't struggle, don't swim against the tide. Go along with it; and if you drown nevertheless, well, that's an easier death after all. They will tell you about economic independence and independent identity. Forget the words. If Draupadi had been economically independent, you think their stories would have been different? No, these are

> things that have been voluntarily surrendered, consciously abandoned, because that is the only way to survive. (137)

Kalpana, in *The Binding Vine*, is another woman who became a victim of the societal/social norms and customs despite her being financially independent. Regarding this Sarabjit Sandhu says: "In spite of the educational opportunities and economic independence, women are surrendered by domestic injustice and the crude customs of our society."[9]

Kalpana was an independent young woman who was fearless and unmindful of the restrictions and constraints of the social norms that bound women. She dressed the way she liked but her worried mother warned her not to "paint and flaunt" herself or else boys in the colonies, "like dogs panting after bitches," (146) would not leave her. But Kalpana paid no heed to what her mother had told her. Shakutai, her mother, blamed her when she was raped, "'I'm not afraid of anyone' she used to say. That's why this happened to her . . . women must know fear" (148). This is nothing but society's way of putting the blame on woman. In today's modern age also, such tradition goes on like a legacy where a rapist is set scot-free and rape victims are blamed in most communities. The condition is more so in Indian society and hence, Indian women are still far away to declare bravely like Virginia Woolf who says aloud: "Food, house and clothing are mine forever. Therefore not merely do effort and labour cease, but also hatred and bitterness. I need not hate any man; he cannot hurt me. I need not flatter any man; he has nothing to give me."[10]

In our society, women, despite everything, still need men and at all times, need to be behind men by pretending and acting even if they don't believe in doing so. Saru in *The Dark Holds No Terrors* speaks from her own bitter experience:

> And so you must pretend that you're not smart as you really are, not as competent as you are, not as rational as you are, and as strong as either. You can nag, complain, henpeck, whine, moan but you can never be strong. That's a wrong which will never be forgotten. (137)

Women, in most Western countries, if they are financially independent, can live and do whatever they like, unmindful of men and the social norms. Whereas, in our country, women have to care about what others think and say: "At present, even when a woman is bearing the entire economic burden of the family, she is not treated as the head of the household."[11]

However, there are some positive influences of financial independence on women's amelioration. It helps to free them from their total dependence syndrome to a certain extent. In *Roots and Shadows,* for instance, Akka, the married sister of the protagonist's father came back after the death of her husband. Being childless, she inherited all the money and the properties of her husband. Since that day, she became the authority of the family—adults and children alike. Indu recalls:

> Since the day Akka had come back a rich childless widow to her brother's house, she had maintained absolute control over her brother's children. Kaka, even after becoming a grandfather, could be reduced to a red-faced stuttering schoolboy by Akka's venomous tongue. (22)

Because of her financial position, Akka could exercise her control over her brother's family. If, on the other hand, she happened to come back childless and dependent, instead of the queen like authority she's enjoying, she might have got nothing but a parasitic treatment as in the case of Saru's grandmother in *The Dark Holds No Terrors* who came back with two girls when her husband had deserted her. Her father looked after them and got the girls married. "But there had been obviously the burden of being unwanted, of being a dependent" (70). Had she been rich and prosperous like Indu's grandmother, her condition would not be the same. On the contrary, Akka who was old, weak and a widow, managed to live a life of authority, and this may be attributed to the wealth and properties she possessed.

Before her death, she had given all her money and property to Indu. Everyone in the family, her Kakas and Kakis, had different opinions as to how the money should be used. Mini, her cousin, confided to her about what's going on in the family:

> They want to settle all the money matters. And about the property as well. I think they are going to have a partition. And they want to know what you're going to do with Akka's money? (91)

Indu finally makes up her mind that she cannot enrich herself with Akka's money; instead she resolves that she would use the money to pay for Mini's wedding. It may not serve the interest and purpose of every family member, but ultimately they all have to agree or submit to Indu's resolutions. This is, perhaps, because of her new-found financial position that makes them listen to and respect her decision: otherwise, who will care to allow a young woman to make, perhaps, the most important decision of the family where women (not even Akka, in her heyday) are not allowed to participate in family discussions. Here, financial position of Indu works positively to express her freedom as an individual. M Mani Meitei rightly observes, "Money plays an important role to bridge the gender gap and to raise one's position."[12]

In *That Long Silence*, Jeeja, Jaya's maid-servant, exercises control over her money. She maintains her family single-handedly as her drunkard husband lives with his second wife. Her husband comes to take money from her regularly. Once she refuses to give money, and that day he goes to Jaya and takes his wife's monthly pay without her knowledge. As soon as Jeeja comes to know about it, she tells Jaya, "Don't ever give my husband any of my pay" (51). Jeeja here exercises her right over the money because it's her own. In this sense, she is much better off than Smita in *The Dark Holds No Terrors* who belongs to higher class than her. Unlike Jeeja, Smita has to depend on the meagre amount of money tightly sanctioned by her husband who doesn't care to provide any allowances of her feelings and sentiments. As discussed in chapter II, one can see the predicament and unpleasant situation she faces just for a small amount like one hundred rupees. For this, she has to ask her childhood friend when they have a get-together after a long time:

> Can you give me a hundred? You know I came here for my nephew's thread ceremony. He gave just enough to buy a small gift for the boy. But I had to buy a sari for my sister-in-law as well. It would have looked very mean if I hadn't. All the others did it. And

> four of us, the children and I, staying here for nearly a month. He doesn't understand these things. He takes it for granted I'm welcomed here. Now if I tell him I've bought a sari as a gift, he'll be furious. So I thought if you lend me a hundred . . . I haven't paid the shop for it as yet . . . I will return the money to you later. (118-19)

Had Smita been financially independent, she would not have faced such a situation. What she tells Saru, "You don't know how lucky you are not to have to ask anyone for money. If you knew my problems" (119) speaks volumes of what she is going through. Jeeja, on the other hand, can take decision and exercise her money independent of her husband.

Women in all cultures, Eastern or Western, suffer as a group under the male-dominated society, though with varying degree. What Simone de Beauvoir has stated still holds true in the present society too: "In the economic sphere men and women can almost be said to make up two castes; other things being equal, the former hold the better jobs, get higher wages, and have more opportunity for success than their new competitors."[13] Even in a developed country like the US, women do not share the same opportunity with men on equal footing. "Women's low income which reflects low paying jobs, remains at about sixty percent below men."[14] From the very beginning to the present age, women have not been given enough encouragement and equal opportunities to be financially independent. Most women in India are housewives, bearing and rearing children, looking after the old and the family chores. They hardly get time for themselves. They have to think twice before they take up any job because the workplace is more often located away from the home, she is forced to carry the "double-burden" of home maker and wage earner or be only the home maker and reconcile herself to the traditional gender role where the "work" has still not achieved the same value as the work performed outside.[15]

In some traditional societies, women, especially daughters-in-law, are openly discouraged from joining any profession because it is considered disgraceful for the family if women are allowed to go out for work of any kind. This is a fine example of how patriarchy works to the suppression and relegation of women by making them believe that all the private and unproductive work is meant for women and all the public and profitable work is meant for men. It is an unfortunate situation that the present-day modern society, despite its progress and development in various fields, still allows to exist such age-old, outdated and imbalanced notions.

In some Western countries like England and the USA, housewives are paid for maintenance but in India, women are being exploited at all levels. No doubt, our constitution has made and provided laws to improve women's lot, but the mindset of the people is still unchanged and hence their suffering. For example, the constitution has provided women rights to inherit their parental properties. If any daughter fights for her right to property against her parents or brothers, when they fail to give her share, society condemns the woman. Because of social stigma, society remains unchanged. Mukta Gupta rightly comments: "An educated Indian woman today has been granted social and economic freedom. The constitution has granted her equal right with man. But very few women even today have the courage to defy tradition and to challenge injustice."[16]

Even when women are economically independent, they are not free to use their own money the way they like. Shantha Krishnaswamy writes: "Economic independence is obviously not enough. Family and marriage laws bind her completely. The norm of legal equality guaranteeing her the same quantum of civic and political rights exists mainly on papers."[17]

"Equal pay for equal work," though it's there in our Constitution, it is not in practice, especially in rural areas where men are paid more than the women for the equal work. This is another exploitation of women in patriarchal society. The domestication and confinement of women add to their oppression and victimization. In Indian society, as pointed out by Malladi Subbama, the condition of the housewives is more pathetic than that of the slaves as the latter are paid for their work and hence earn an income of their own. She observes, "a slave is purchased with money. But a woman goes into slavery paying the husband in the shape of dowry. Is it not horrible slavery?"[18]

If women are to liberate themselves, they need to change their mindset regarding the norms and roles society has dictated for them to follow, besides being educated and economically independent. Rashmi Gaur says, "The changing social dynamics had brought about a change in the socio-economic-educational-rights-awareness among the women, but they still have to create a niche for them."[19] Shashi Deshpande too feels that economic independence is the pre-condition of women's emancipation, though it is not necessarily the only solution. Summing up her opinion she tells in one of her interviews:

> It is not enough for the women to be educated and economically independent. . . . Education and economic independence are the tools. They can help you, they may not, and you may be both educated and though economically independent and you may still be bound and wrapped by conventions and brainwashed by the centuries of conditioning. . . . To me it is more important to liberate yourself but even after that you are still living in a society where everybody is not thinking the way you are. It does not necessarily mean that you are going to be free, but then you are able to at least take the first step, which is for me always the most important step.[20]

Household chores and child care should be shared by both instead of taking them as solely women's domain. Sri Nani Mahanta opines: "Women constitute half of the world's population, yet they are not given a chance to utilize one half of the total resources. The situation is more fluid in a country like India where women are considered to be species meant for looking after household activities and serving the members of the family."[21]

Since it is not possible to change the socio-cultural and traditional set-up of our society overnight, it is necessary to try to change at least our own concepts first instead of waiting for the others to change. This "desire to go beyond what you see and reach the truth"[22] is what is important for women's liberation. Proper education and training combined with economic liberation and strong self-determination are called for women's liberation. Women should be treated on an equal footing with man. Women also should neither think and work that they are of a lesser breed nor are they sexually, bodily or otherwise subservient to man.

They should place themselves outside the sexual disparity and thus overcome psychodynamic problems and issues that keep them handicapped. At the same time, man's attitude towards women needs to be revamped on the basis of equality and sharing. Only then economic independence of women will bear fruit.

NOTES

1. Qtd. Vinita Kaul, "An Economic Perspective" *Women and the Wind of Change* (New Delhi, Gyan, 2000), 163.
2. Virginia Woolf, *Three Guineas* (New York: Harcourt, Brace and World, 1963).
3. Shashi Deshpande, "In First Person" *Writing from the Margin and Other Essays*, 15.
4. N. Sharada Iyer, "Socialisation and Gender Construction in Shashi Deshpande's Novels," T.M.J. Indra Mohan, ed.. *Shashi Deshpande: A Critical Spectrum*, 43.
5. Iqbal Kaur, "Prefatory Note," Iqbal Kaur, ed., *Perspectives on Kamala Das's Poetry* (New Delhi: Intellectual, 1995), VII.
6. S. Anandlakshmi, "The Female Child in a Family Setting," *The Indian Journal of Social Work*, No. 1, Vol. LII, Jan. 1991: 31.
7. Nalinabh Tripathi, "Gender Identity and Inner Space in *The Dark Holds No Terrors*," R.S. Pathak, ed., *The Fiction of Shashi Deshpande*, 44.
8. Premila Paul, "*The Dark Holds No Terrors*: A Call for Confrontation," R.S. Pathak, ed., *The Fiction of Shashi Deshpande*, 31.
9. Sarabjit Sandhu, "Introduction," *The Novels of Shashi Deshpande* (New Delhi: Prestige, 1991), 9.
10. Virginia Woolf, *A Room of One's Own*, 46.
11. N. Jusha Rao, "Socio-Economic Needs of Women—Challenges Ahead," *Women in Developing Society* (New Delhi: Ashish, 1983), 161.
12. M. Mani Meitei, "Subverting Phallogocentrism: Feminine Discourse in *Roots and Shadows*," R.S. Pathak, ed., *The Fiction of Shashi Deshpande*, 83.
13. Simone de Beauvoir, "Introduction" *The Second Sex*, XXVI.
14. Vinita Kaul, "An Economic Perspective," *Women and the Wind of Change*, 166.
15. *Ibid.*

16. Mukta Gupta, "Girl Child: A Neglected Dimension," *Issues Related to Women*, 99.
17. Shantha Krishnaswamy, "Conclusion: And She Shall Arise," *The Woman in Indian Fiction in English* (New Delhi. Ashish, 1984), 359.
18. Malladi Subbama, "To Whom Are We Slaves?" *Women, Tradition and Culture*, 4.
19. Rashmi Gaur, "Images of Indian Woman in Shashi Deshpande's *That Long Silence*—Stereotypes, Myths and Realities," *Pegasus* Vol. II (Dec. 2002/Jan. 2003): 39.
20. Pallavi Thakur, "An Interview with Shashi Deshpande," *The Quest*, 17/2, June (2003): 67.
21. Sri Nani Mahanta, "Economic Reforms and Marginalisation of Women," *Status of Women and Social Change* (Guwahati: Women's Studies Research Centre, 1996), 129.
22. Pallavi Thakur, 67.

Conclusion

Shashi Deshpande as a feminist writer projects women's lives and problems from the perspective of a woman. Her feminism, as already discussed in chapter II, is quite different from Western radical feminism which often considers man at the root of women's suffering, oppression and deprivation. She neither believes in the concept that her women characters should go out of their way, shouting slogans, protesting and revolting against men nor blaming men as the sole cause of women's subordination and suffering. Her writings reflect delicate issues like rape within and without marriage, gender disparities and various problems faced by women as a group in a male-dominated society, yet they are far from being prejudiced and biased as often found in some writings of both men and women when they write about their opposite sex. She points out women's blind spots along with that of their male counterparts. Such objective and realistic representation of women helps us to study and analyze women's genuine problems, their causes and remedies from a fresh perspective. This is one very significant achievement and contribution of Shashi Deshpande as a novelist.

Chapter II has also endeavoured to study Shashi Deshpande's concerns and predilections as a novelist. The interplay of the past and the present, using first and third person narrations is an effective technique employed by the novelist. This technique enables the novelist to represent women's life and sufferings realistically and objectively which is also her main preoccupation. Because of this, her treatment of women characters is clouded with darkness, but a close look reveals the silver lining too. If she depicts a dark picture of the contemporary women's lives extensively, it may be because she would like to mirror the actual happenings and conditions of the society where women are subjected to hardships and suffering. Here she seems to share the views of Joyce Carol Oates when she says, regarding the task of an artist, "I wish the world were a prettier place but I wouldn't be honest as a writer if I ignored the actual conditions around me."[1] In this chapter, the novelist's attempt to deconstruct man-made ideas, rules and system is also made. Men of all ages, consciously or unconsciously, conspire to relegate and push women to the margin while they enjoy every advantage and privilege at the centre. In our country, because of the social and traditional factors, women's exploitation is multi-layered. Shashi Deshpande, like Anita Desai who focuses mainly on the disturbed and hypersensitive women of middle class and Shobha De who exposes the reality, plight and prejudices of elite class women, unfolds the sexual politics at all levels and in all sections of the society.

The study has attempted to study the novelist's awareness of women's problems and predicaments, their said and unsaid thoughts and feelings, their dilemmas, hopes and frustrations as reflected in her novels. As a woman writer, she tries to unfold the untold stories of women, especially those belonging to the middle class who is walking on the tightrope between tradition and modernity. These educated, young women are highly aware of the prevailing customs and traditions that bind them and also deeply conscious of their rights as individuals. As a result, they live an ambivalent and self-contradictory life. They suffer mainly because they are trapped in a puzzling maze created by the labyrinths of traditional and modern values/outlooks. Their inner conflict and their battle within create a lot of tension, confusion and frustration that force them to live a life of suppression and alienation.

Alienation is another factor that keeps human relationships strangulated in modern society. Edmund Fuller rightly states, "Man suffers not only from wars, persecution, famine and ruin but from inner problems—isolation, randomness and meaninglessness in his way of existence."[2] In Deshpande's novels, the theme of alienation is widely dispersed, especially in her later novels—*A Matter of Time* and *Moving On*. One of the main causes of alienation is lack of communication, as discussed in chapter II.

Modern civilization has brought news from far off corners of the world within seconds but we fail to know what happens to our near and dear ones and next door neighbours who have been with us for years. Women protagonists in the novels of Shashi Deshpande suffer from double alienation—alienation from self and alienation from others/society. They are alienated from their selves as they are torn apart between the traditional norms and their modern concepts. The second alienation from others/society may be attributed to their lack of participation, initiation and communication. For example, Saru and Manohar in *The Dark Holds No Terrors* might have solved their problems and differences, had Saru opened and talked to her husband in time.

The exclusion of women in important discussions and activities in and outside family, marriage, childbirth, strict role-division between men and women, separate social and moral codes of conduct, etc. further alienate women. Thus women's alienation culminates in their identity crisis. To combat such alienation and identity crisis, Deshpande seems to suggest the need to have solidarity among women, instead of their being hostile to one another, and build male-female bonding with understanding for a better and more secure life for both, based on common welfare besides encouraging women to share things, take initiatives, to communicate and participate in domestic and social activities. Both men and women should try to bridge the gap instead of building walls between them as done by Shripati and his wife in *A Matter of Time* who have not been on talking terms for more than thirty-five years.

Women need moral support from their men in their attempt to liberate themselves. Geeta, in Rama Mehta's *Inside the Haveli*, perhaps, goes through everything and manages to reform the traditional people of the 'Haveli' slowly but surely in her own way because she gets the much-needed support, encouragement and understanding of her husband who says:

> I know, it is difficult for you here, but, Geeta, by being depressed, you will not change things. . . . This life in purdah is not meant for you. Help me to try and see what you could do in this atmosphere.

> You must always have confidence in me that I will support you in whatever you decide to do.[3]

Unfortunately, Deshpande's heroines do not have such understanding husbands and they find consolation and companionship in other men. This leads them to develop extra-marital affairs with other men as in the cases of Saru and Boozie in *The Dark Holds No Terrors*, Indu and Naren in *Roots and Shadows*, Jaya and Kamat in *That Long Silence*, Urmila and Bhasker in *The Binding Vine*, though the novelist does not let such an extra marital relationship go further and develop into a full-fledged one. The revelation of Boozie as a gay, the sudden and untimely deaths of Naren and Kamat and the conscious departure of Urmi seem to say that Deshpande does not consider such relationships as ideal alternatives.

In Chapter IV the focus is on how Deshpande's women characters react and respond to various oppressive systems of patriarchy as they have experienced growth and development of their personality from being immature, inexperienced to mature, experienced individuals. First, like stern feminists, the protagonists are ready to smite everything that threatens their independence. In the second phase, they suffer from post-marriage syndromes—submissiveness, timidity, selfless sacrifice and total silence—syndromes most married women in Indian society undergo. They imprison their educated and modern outlook in their self-created shells and follow the dictates of the society much against their will. They are not happy and satisfied with their life as they feel suffocated because of their bottled-up emotions and feelings. They take a long time before they finally self-examine and attain self-discovery, which according to the novelist is the basis of women's emancipation, and this constitutes the last phase of the growth of their personality.

The next chapter studies and analyzes various problems and predicaments faced by women, how and why women are being suppressed and victimized in our society. As discussed in the earlier chapter, the novelist is highly sensitive to the inequalities and injustices meted out to women in the name of culture and tradition.

The novelist realizes that women as a group suffer not because of their sex but because of the social and cultural attitudes attached to their sex by the patriarchal society. Women's suffering starts from womb and ends in their tombs. Most of the problems arise because men are not ready to accept women as their fellow beings, companions and individuals, other than being their daughters, wives and mothers. The need to deconstruct and dismantle such traditional and outdated mindset of people, both educated and uneducated alike that reduces women to merely sexual objects, child-bearing machines and twenty-four hours' help-maids has been emphasized in her novels.

Further, the chapter also discusses how the novels of Shashi Deshpande expose various social, cultural and gender inequalities in all sections of the society. An in-depth study of how social and religious institutions perpetuate women's victimization in a country like India has also been made. Marriage, for example, becomes bondage where women have to surrender and sacrifice endlessly, even their names and surnames, habits, hopes and aspirations, careers, etc. Preference of male child and negligence of girl child is very much prevalent in the society. One important reason for this may be the financial factor as already discussed in chapter VI. Parents have to spend a lot of money on bringing them up, educating them and finally getting them married without any return. On the other hand, they enrich themselves with the money or the dowry they get from their sons' marriage. If women are earning, the attitudes towards them may change in the course of time. In this way, women can be equally responsible on both domestic and social fronts. Only then the preference for male child will be replaced. Here the novelist stresses the importance of education that would change and question the age-old man-made concepts and notions that were to magnify man's image by relegating women to secondary status.

Many eminent personalities and feminists emphasize imparting of education as the solution to most problems of life faced by women (and men). We need the kind of education that creates awareness and consciousness among women of the existing social and cultural imbalance. Acquiring degrees and bookish knowledge should not be the only aim of education. Education should be able to change men and women internally and externally, and be able to achieve socially beneficial goals for both men and women. Women's education will bring about changes in the society while making them aware of their rights and privileges, and of their role and responsibility in the society, and of removing social evils and gender discrimination. Swami Vivekananda once said: "educate your women first and leave them for we want that education by which character is formed, strength of mind is increased, the intellect is expanded and by which one can stand on one's own feet. With such education women will solve their own problems."[4]

Education is all the more important for women to face the multi-layered problems and sufferings they have gone through under patriarchy. They have been excluded and isolated from various private and public activities for ages, and education is the only outlet from their secluded life. What African feminist Buchi Emecheta writes about African women is applicable to all women, emphasizing the role of women in the family and society: "I want very much to further the education of women in Africa, because I know that education really helps them to rear a generation. It is true that if one educates a woman, one educates a community: whereas if we educate a man one educates a man."[5]

Unlike most of Anita Desai's heroines who, unable to face the harsh realities of life and the subjective treatment under patriarchy, seek to find an escape either by committing suicide as in the case of Maya in *Cry the Peacock*, Sita in *Where Shall We Go This Summer*?[6] or seeking space outside the society by residing in a secluded place as in the case of Nanda Kaul in *Fire on the Mountain*, Deshpande's heroines do not seem to believe in this narrow freedom if one can call it freedom at all. They search for a broader and deeper freedom demanding their place and position in the society almost equal to their male counterparts. In fact, each of her protagonists has struggled for a long time, undergone the birth-pangs before she finally gives birth to a new liberated self. Here, liberation does not mean walking out of relationship, marriage or society as Deshpande, when asked why her women, who are so troubled by patriarchy, don't rebel, replies:

> The problem is that rebelling is generally understood to mean walking out on a marriage (the echoes of the door Nora banged behind her seem to haunt us!), the problem lies in thinking that walking out is a liberating process. Whereas, to me, it is always clear that an understanding of oneself is what really liberates, it is this that opens out a number of possibilities. To walk out, or away, is to carry the old self with oneself.[7]

It is observed that Deshpande's women characters constantly fight not only against the oppressive system outside but also within themselves with their inner conflicts. Towards the end of the novels, these women come out of their inner turmoil and are ready to face anyone and any situation without any fear, insecurity and hesitation. All her novels end with hope not for just survival but for living a meaningful and better life.

Most of Deshpande's heroines engage themselves, at the very beginning of her novels, in introspection of their past lives; they study and analyze their problems and at the end, they discover their true self. Saru in *The Dark Holds No Terrors* has been afraid and frightened of the dark, of failure and rejection. She turns her back to the problems and silently endures with constant fear. At last, she is no longer afraid of the dark, "the dark holds no terrors" as she asserts herself. In *Roots and Shadows*, Indu is able to realize towards the end that the house has been a trap, binding her to the past, she has to move from (here, the house becomes the symbol of old values and tradition). She is able to find her 'roots' as an individual and differentiate them from the 'shadows' she has been clinging to all the past years. She feels free but not detached as she has "cut away all the unnecessary, uneven edges" (44). At last, she too, is able to assert herself and drive away all kinds of fear: "How can I live without fear . . . fears of being unloved, misjudged, misunderstood, displeasing. Without the fear of failure" (44).

In the same way, Jaya is able to break "that long silence" and head for a better life, full of hope and positive thoughts as she says, "But we can always hope. Without that, life would be impossible. And if there is anything I know now it is this: life has always to be made possible" (193). In *The Binding Vine*, Urmi who has been grieving over the death of her baby daughter, discovers the suffering of others—of her long dead mother-in-law, of Akka, of Kalpana, Shakutai, Sulu, etc. In spite of all their suffering, they are bound by "the binding vine" of love and compassion. This novel explores the theme of female solidarity to a greater extent.

The novel, *A Matter of Time* also ends with love, sympathy and compassion. Aru finally accepts her father's wandering life with "dignity and strength." (42) In *Small Remedies*, as the title suggests, the protagonist Madhu, who has been in great despair over the death of her only son Aditya, is able to find some "small remedies" that can heal the wounds and sufferings of life. *Moving On* ends with a desire of the protagonist, Jiji, to move on with life despite so many deaths and sufferings.

Self-discovery and self-realization become very important as that can turn the whole situation. All this leads to a new beginning, a new life with hopes. Whether they will be successful or not in their battle of life, whether their solution to their problems are right or wrong, is not what the novelist is trying to project; hers is to show their will, determination and spirit to have a good fight against all odds. Like a true soldier, they prepare themselves for the battles of life without relying on others. To have and develop such spirit is what is needed for our society. As we have observed, all the protagonists of Deshpande are well-educated and most of them are economically independent when the novels open, but they are still subjected to sexual violence, gender discrimination, unequal and unjust treatment in the society before they attain self-realization and liberate themselves. This infers that being educated and financially independent is not the only requisite for attainment of women's emancipation, especially in a society like that of India where women's oppression is often multi-layered as discussed in chapter VI. Most Indian women novelists are concerned with the depiction of women's suffering—women as a sexual group. Anita Desai, Shashi Deshpande, Shobha De highlight women's plight—women of all castes and classes. For example, Mikki in Shobha De's *Sisters* suffers very badly, in spite of her education and financial position, at the dominating hands of her husband, Binny Malhotra. What the husband says very proudly by quoting the family's tradition while he himself enjoys many affairs may be observed:

> In our family women are trained to obey their husbands . . . you will never I repeat, never, question me or complain where I go, what I do, when and with whom, is my business . . . your job is to look beautiful. I told you that when I married you. Buy clothes. Buy jewellery. Go to the beauty parlour. Play bridge. Learn golf. Attend cooking classes. That is all. But no question—you don't have the right.[8]

The same age-old notions and attitudes are still observed by both men and women, educated or uneducated. Hence, the need to change such out-dated and gender-biased ideas.

The study also explores Deshpande's efforts to bring to light women's victimization, marginalization and exploitation at all levels—physical, psychological, emotional, social, political, cultural and domestic—under patriarchy. She goes on to expose how from laymen to the most revered learned men of all ages, barring a few, consciously or unconsciously join hands in degrading women with the ideas, opinions and institutions formulated and established by them. The novelist also shows how men and women today are victims of such biased visions and discrepancies. The novelist's sympathetic and objective treatment of her male characters drives home the point that Deshpande's feminism does not target individual men but exposes the system.

Deshpande's awareness of women's life and problems makes her probe into the depth of their psyche so troubled by patriarchy and also by their own follies and weaknesses as individuals. She seems to urge women to assert themselves, raise their voice and fight against all forms of oppression in the way best suited to their situation instead of bearing it stoically and silently. They should learn to say "no" and put a full stop to their suffering. Self-examination and introspection of how, where and why they went wrong would be the road to women's self-discovery. It is high time women learned to rely on themselves as individuals instead of depending on their fathers, brothers, husbands and sons, though there is room for mutual help and co-operation between men and women. Yes, it is true that patriarchal system binds them and curbs their freedom but it is upto them whether they would submit to it or fight against it. For this, women need proper education, economic independence and self-reliance. In the end, women like Saru, Indu, Jaya, Urmi, Sumi, Madhu and Jiji are able to liberate themselves from the clutches of patriarchy and their self-created shells because they attain all the above-mentioned qualities but sadly there are so many Shakutais, Sulus, Jeejas, Nayanas etc. who are still struggling and suffering because of the lack of the same.

Lastly, Shashi Deshpande as a feminist writer bears no stamp of a separatist stance as observed in chapter II. She is quite different from radical and militant feminists that discard all established social and cultural values. Her reaction and opposition does not target social institutions like marriage or roles like motherhood, but the endless restrictions and constraints, the strict role-division, numerous expectations, surrender and sacrifices imposed on women by the patriarchy. As a woman novelist, Deshpande realizes the impracticability of planting Western Feminism in Indian soil. Her feminism is moderate, considerate, sensible and context-bound. Her emphasis on the need to stay within relationship and at the same time her insistence on being self-independent, her attempts to synthesize tradition and modernity and reorientation of modern Feminism in conformity with Indian culture for a well-balanced, meaningful and harmonious relationship between men and women in the society by dismantling all imbalances earn her a niche among the Indian women writers writing in English. The significance, relevance and practicability of her feminist concern, reflected in her novels and the humanistic and universal approaches to which she is committed, invariably underscore the success of Shashi Deshpande as a novelist.

NOTES

1. Qtd. Sushila Singh, "Joyce Carol Oates: The Women Question in her Exploration of the Contemporary Human Condition," *Feminism: Theory, Criticism, Analysis*, 131.
2. Qtd. L. Manjula Davidson, "Alienation in Indian Novels in English," *The Quest*, No. 2, Vol. 20, Dec. 2006: 19.

3. Rama Mehta, *Inside the Haveli* (New Delhi: Penguin India, 1996), 52-53.
4. Qtd. Prasanna Sree Sathupati, "Conflict and Identity in Shashi Deshpande's Novels," R.K. Dhawan, ed., *Indian Women Novelists*, Vol. 4, set III (New Delhi: Prestige, 1995), 18.
5. Qtd. Toril Moi, *Sexual/Textual Politics: Feminist Literary Theory* (London: Routledge, 1995), 98.
6. Anita Desai, *Where Shall We Go This Summer?* (Delhi: Vision, 1982).
7. Shashi Deshpande, "Writing from the Margin," *Writing from the Margin and Other Essays*, 159.
8. Shobha De, *Sisters* (New Delhi: Penguin, 1992), 116.

Bibliography

Primary Sources

Deshpande, Shashi. *The Dark Holds No Terrors.* 1980. New Delhi: Penguin, 1990.

_____. *If I Die Today*. Delhi: Vikas, 1982.

_____. *Roots and Shadows*. New Delhi: Disha, 1983.

_____. *Come Up and Be Dead.* Delhi: Vikas, 1983.

_____. *That Long Silence.* 1988. New Delhi: Penguin, 1989.

_____. *The Binding Vine*. 1993. New Delhi: Penguin, 2001.

_____. *A Matter of Time.* New Delhi: Penguin, 1996.

_____. *Small Remedies.* New Delhi: Penguin, 2000.

_____. *Moving On*. New Delhi: Penguin, 2004.

_____. *The Intrusion and Other Stories.* New Delhi: Penguin Books, 1993.

_____. *Collected Stories*. 2 Vols. New Delhi: Penguin India, 2003.

Secondary Sources

Adhikari, Madhumalati. "Defying Patriarchy: Female Protagonists in Virginia Woolf's *Mrs. Dalloway*, Toni Morrison's *Beloved* and Anita Desai's *Clear Light of Day*," *Points of View*, No. 1, Vol. II., summer 1995.

Aikant, Satish C. "Culture and Decolonization" Satish C. Aikant ed. *Critical Spectrum: Essays in Literary Culture,* Delhi: Pencraft, 2004.

Allott, Miriam. *Novelists on the Novels.* London: Routledge and Kegan Paul, 1959.

Anandlakshmi, S. "The Female Child in a Family Setting *The Indian Journal of Social Work*, No. 1, Vol. LII, Jan, 1991.

Bai, K. Meera. *Women's Voices: The Novels of Indian Writers.* New Delhi: Prestige, 1996.

Bair, Deirdre. "Introduction to the Vintage Edition," *The Second Sex,* Trans and ed. H.M. Parshley, Rpt. New York: Vintage Books, 1989.

Bala, Suman. *Women in the Novels of Shashi Deshpande*. New Delhi: Khosla, 2002.

Beauvoir, Simone De. *The Second Sex*, trans. and ed. H.M. Parshley. Rpt. New York: Vintage, 1989.

Bharat, Meenakshi, ed. *Desert in Bloom: Contemporary Indian Women's Fiction in English*. Delhi: Pencraft International, 2004.

Bilefsky, Dan. "Now, 'honour suicide' in Turkey." *Times of India*, 13 July 2006.

Carden, Maren Lockwood. *The New Feminist Movement.* New York: Russell Sage Foundation, 1974.

Coward, Rosalind. "This Novel Changes Women's Lives: Are Women's Novels Feminist Novels," *Feminist Review*, 5 (1980).

Cixous, Helene. "The Laugh of the Medusa," Mary Eagleton, ed., *Feminist Literary Theory: A Reader*. 320-22.

_____. "Castration or Decapitation?" Mary Eagleton, ed., *Feminist Literary Theory: A Reader*. 322-24.

Das, Kamala. "My Story," *My Stories*. New Delhi: Sterling, 1976. 108-9.

_____. "An Introduction." Vinayak Krishna Gokak, ed., *The Golden Treasury of Indo-Anglian Poetry (1828-1965)*. Delhi: Pencraft, 1998. 272-73.

Dhawan, R.K. ed. *Indian Women's Novelists.* 18 Vols. New Delhi: Prestige, 1991-1995.

Davidson, L. Manjula. "Alienation in Indian Novels in English," *The Quest*, No. 2, Vol. 20, Dec. 2006: 19-28.

_____. De, Shobha. *Sisters*. New Delhi: Penguin, 1992.

_____. Desai, Anita. *Voices in the City*. Delhi: Orient, 1965.

_____. *Cry, the Peacock*. Delhi: Orient, 1980.

_____. *Where Shall We Go This Summer?* Delhi: Vision, 1982.

_____. *Fire on the Mountain*. London: Vintage, 1999.

De, Shobha. *Sisters.* New Delhi: Penguin, 1992.

Deshpande, Shashi. "The Dilemma of the Woman Writer," R.S. Pathak, ed., *The Fiction of Shashi Deshpande*. 229-31.

_____. *Writing from the Margin and Other Essays*. New Delhi: Penguin, 2003.

Donovan, Josephine, ed. *Feminist Literary Criticism: Explorations in Theory*. Kentucky: University Press, 1975.

Eagleton, Mary, ed. *Feminist Literary Theory: A Reader*. Rpt. New Delhi: Saujanya, 1999.

Foreman, Anne. *Marxism and Psychoanalysis*: London: Pluto, 1977.

Forrester, Viviane. "'What Women's Eyes See': New French Feminists," Mary Eagleton, ed., *Feminist Literary Theory: A Reader.* Rpt. Massachusetts, Blackwell, 1996. 56-58.

Friedan, Betty. *The Feminine Mystique*. Rpt. Harmondsworth: Penguin, 1971.

Geetha, Gangadharan. "Denying the Otherness" (Interview), R.S. Pathak, ed. *The Fiction of Shashi Deshpande.* 251-55.

Gaur, Rashmi. *Women's Writing: Some Facets.* New Delhi: Sarup, 2003.

Greer, Germaine. *The Female Eunuch.* Rpt. St. Alabama: Paladin, 1976.

Guerin, et al. *A Handbook of Critical Approaches to Literature.* New York: OUP, 1999.

Gupta, Mukta. *Issues Related to Women.* New Delhi: Sarup, 2000.

_____. "Girl Child: A Neglected Dimension," *Issues Related to Women.*

Hardy, Thomas. *Tess of the D'Urbervilles.* Rpt. London: Macmillan, 1949.

Holmstrom, Lakshmi. "Shashi Deshpande Talks to Lakshmi Holmstrom" (Interview), R.S. Pathak, ed. *The Fiction of Shashi Deshpande.* 242-50.

Humm, Maggie, *The Dictionary of Feminist Theory.* London: Harvester Wheatsheaf, 1995.

Indira, S. "A Bond or a Burden? A Study of Shashi Deshpande's *The Binding Vine*" *Indian Women Novelists,* R.K. Dhawan, ed., Set III Vol. 6, New Delhi: Prestige, 1995. 21-27.

Iyer, N. Sharada. "Socialisation and Gender Construction in Shashi Deshpande's Novels," T.M.J. Indra Mohan, ed., *Shashi Deshspande: A Critical Spectrum.* New Delhi: Atlantic, 2004. 42-48.

Jaidev, "Problematizing Feminism," Sushila Singh, ed., *Feminism and Recent Fiction in English.* New Delhi: Prestige, 1991. 48-63.

Jain, Jasbir. "Men in the Minds of Women: Women Writers and Male Narrators in the Fiction of Nayantara Sahgal, Anita Desai and Githa Hariharan" Meenakshi Bharat, ed., *Desert in Bloom: Contemporary Indian Women's Fiction in English.* 43-58.

Jardine, Alice. *Gynesis: Configurations of Women and Modernity.* Ithaca: Cornell University Press, 1986.

Jung, C.G. *Aspects of the Feminine,* trans. R.F.C. Hull. London: Routledge and Kegan Paul, 1982.

Kaul, Vinita. "An Economic Perspective," *Women and the Wind of Change.* New Delhi: Gyan, 2000.

Kaur, Iqbal. "Prefatory Note," Iqbal Kaur, ed., *Perspective on Kamala Das's Poetry* .New Delhi: Intellectual, 1995.

Kelly, Joan. *Women, History, Theory: The Essays of Joan Kelly.* Chicago: University of Chicago Press, 1984.

Khan, Nazneen. "Woman 'Made' Woman in the Novels of Shashi Deshpande," *Pegasus—A Journal of Literary and Critical Studies.* Vol. IV, Jan.-Dec. (2005): 57-62.

Krishnaswamy, Shantha. "Conclusion: And She Shall Arise" *The Woman in Indian Fiction in English.* New Delhi. Ashish, 1984.

Kudchedkar, Shirin. "Feminist Literary Criticism: The Ground Work," *Journal of Literary Criticism,* Vol. VIII, no. 1, June 1996.

Larrington, Carolyne, ed. *The Women's Companion to Mythology*. London: Harper Collins, 1992.

Light, Alison. "Feminism and the Literary Critic," Mary Eagleton, ed., *Feminism Literary Theory: A Reader*. 242-45.

Lipking, Lawrence. "Aristotle's Sister: A Poetics of Abandonment," *Critical Inquiry*, 10 September 1983.

Mahanta, Sri Nani. "Economic Reforms and Marginalisation of Women," *Status of Women and Social Change*. Guwahati: Women's Studies Research Centre, 1996.

Marder, Herbert. *Feminism and Art: A Study of Virginia Woolf*. Chicago and London: The University of Chicago Press, 1968.

Mehta, Rama. *Inside the Haveli*. New Delhi: Penguin India, 1996.

Meitei, M. Mani. "Feminism and Anita Desai's *Cry, the Peacock* and *Where Shall We Go This Summer*?" P.M. Nayak and S.P. Swain, ed., *Feminism and Indian English Fiction*. Bareilly: Prakash, 1996.

_____. *The Stream of Consciousness Techniques with Special Reference to the Novels of Virginia Woolf*. Diss. Manipur University, 1987.

_____. "Subverting Phallogocentrism: Feminine Discourse in *Roots and Shadows*" R.S. Pathak, ed., *The Fiction of Shashi Deshpande*. 73-85.

Millett, Kate. *Sexual Politics*. Rpt. London: Virago, 1977.

Mill, John Stuart. *The Subjection of Women*. Rpt. Cambridge: The M.I.T. Press, 1989.

Mohan, T.M.J. Indra, ed. *Shashi Deshspande: A Critical Spectrum*. New Delhi: Atlantic, 2004.

Moi Toril, "Feminist Literary Criticism," Ann Jafferson and David Robey, ed., *Modern Literary Theory*. London: B.T. Batsford, 1986.

_____. *Sexual/Textual Politics: Feminist Literary Theory*. London: Routledge, 1995.

Mukherjee, Meenakshi. 21 Feb 2006 < http: // www.Indiaclub. Com /Fiction/Moving On/Review/2>.

Muzumdar, Kalindi. "Women and Violence: A Human Rights Perspective," Shirin K. and Sabiha Al-Issa, eds. *Violence against Women: Women against Violence*. Delhi: Pencraft, 1998. 28-48.

Nayar, Nandini. 5 Aug 2005 < http://www.achuka.co.uk /interviews /deshpande.php/1>.

Nityanandam, Indira, "Assimilation or Alienation: A Study of Monisha in Anita Desai's *Voices in the City* and Geeta in Rama Mehta's *Inside the Haveli*" R.K. Dhawan, ed., *Indian Women Novelists*. Set II, Vol. 1, New Delhi: Prestige, 1993. 69-74.

_____. "Shashi Deshpande's *The Binding Vine*: Silent No More," R.K. Dhawan ed. *Indian Women's Novelists*. Set III Vol. 4 New Delhi: Prestige, 1995. 60-66.

Pandey K.M. "Tearing the Veil: *The Dark Holds No Terrors*," R.S. Pathak, ed., *The Fiction of Shashi Deshpande*. 49-57.

Pathak, R.S. ed. *The Fiction of Shashi Deshpande*. New Delhi: Prestige, 2002.

_____. *Modern Indian Novels in English*. Delhi: Saujanya, 1999.

Paul, Premila. "*The Dark Holds No Terrors*: A Call for Confrontation" R.S. Pathak, ed., *The Fiction of Shashi Deshpande*.

Prakash, Nirmala. "From Feminine to Feminist Consciousness; Shashi Deshpande's *The Stone Women*." T.M.J. Indra Mohan, ed. *Shashi Deshpande: A Critical Spectrum*. New Delhi: Atlantic, 2004. 33-41.

Prasad, Amarnath. ed. *New Lights on Indian Women Novelists in English*. Delhi: Saujanya, 2003.

Pratt, Anis. *Archetypal Pattern in Women's Fiction*. Bloomington: Indiana University Press, 1981.

Rao, N. Jusha. "Socio-Economic Needs of Women—Challenges Ahead," *Women in Developing Society*. New Delhi: Ashish, 1983.

Rao, Vimala Rama, "In Conversation with Shashi Deshpande," R.S. Pathak, ed., *The Fiction of Shashi Deshpande*. 256-59.

Rani, K. Nirupa, "Woman, Society and Religion: Tehmina Durrani's Quest for Identity," *The Literary Criterion*, Vol. xxxviii, 2003, No. 3 and 4. 45-53.

Reddy, Y.S. Sunita, *A Feminist Perspective on the Novels of Shashi Deshpande*. New Delhi: Prestige, 2001.

Register, Cheri. "American Feminist Literary Criticism: A Bibliographical Introduction," Josephine Donovan, ed., *Feminist Literary Criticism: Explorations in Theory*. Kentucky: University Press of Kentucky, 1975.

Riti, M.D., "There's No Looking Back" (Interview) R.S. Pathak, ed., *The Fiction of Shashi Deshpande*. 238-341.

Ruthven, K.K. *Feminist Literary Studies: An Introduction*. London: Cambridge, 1984.

Sahgal, Nayantara. *Storm in Chandigarh*. London: Chatto and Windus, 1969.

Sandhu, Sarabjit. *The Novels of Shashi Deshpande*. New Delhi: Prestige Books, 1991.

Sankranti, Sujata. "No Identity No Self!" Meenakshi Bharat, ed., *Desert in Bloom: Contemporary Indian Women's Fiction in English*. Delhi: Pencraft International, 2004. 223-25.

Sebastian, Mrinalini. *The Novels of Shashi Deshpande in Postcolonial Arguments*. New Delhi: Prestige, 2000.

Shirin, K and Sabiha Al-Issa, eds. *Violence against Women: Women against Violence*. Delhi: Pencraft, 1998.

Showalter, Elaine. "Towards a Feminist Poetics," Phillip Rice and Patricia Waugh, ed., *Modern Literary Theory: A Reader*. Rpt. London: Edward Arnold, 1992. 92-102.

_____. "A Literature of Their Own: British Women Novelists from Bronte to Lessing," Mary Eagleton, ed., *Feminist Literary Theory: A Reader*. Rpt. Massachusetts: Blackwell, 1996. 14-18.

_____. "*The New Feminist Criticism: Essays on Women, Literature and Theory*. New York: Pantheon, 1985.

Singh, Ranjini Jyothi. "Quest for Space and Selfhood in Shashi Deshpande," *Pegasus—A Journal of Literary and Critical Studies*. Vol. IV. Jan.-Dec. 2005: 20-25.

Singh, Sushila. *Feminism: Theory, Criticism, Analysis*. New Delhi: Pencraft International: 1997.

_____. "Recent Trends in Feminist Thought: A Tour De Horizon," *Feminism and Recent Fiction in English*. Sushila Singh, ed. New Delhi: Prestige Books, 1991. 22-36.

Sinha, Kavita. "Women," *Telegraph*, III, Sunday, 6 Oct. 2002.

Sree, S. Prasanna, "An Interview with Shashi Deshpande," Amarnath Prasad, ed., *New Lights on Indian Women Novelists in English*. Delhi: Saujanya, 2003. 89-101.

_____. "Conflict and Identity in Shashi Deshpande's Novels," R.K. Dhawan, ed., *Indian Women Novelists*. Vol. 4, set III. New Delhi: Prestige, 1995.

Subbama, Malladi. "To Whom Are We Slaves?" *Women, Tradition and Culture*.

Swain, S.P. "*Roots and Shadows*: A Feminist Study," R.S. Pathak, ed., *The Fiction of Shashi Deshpande*. 86-96.

Thakur, Pallavi. "An Interview with Shashi Deshpande" *The Quest*, 17/2 June 2003.

Tripathi, Nalinabh. "Gender Identity and Inner Space in *The Dark Holds No Terrors*," R.S. Pathak ed. *The Fiction of Shashi Deshpande*.

Viswanatha, Vanamala. "A Woman's World . . . All the Way!" (Interview) R.S. Pathak ed. *The Fiction of Shashi Deshpande*. New Delhi: Prestige, 2002. 232-37.

Woolf, Virginia. *Granite and Rainbow*. London: The Hogarth Press, 1958.

_____. "'Professions for Women' The Death of the Moth" Mary Eagleton, ed., *Feminist Literary Theory: A Reader*. Rpt Massachusetts: Blackwell, 1996.

_____. *A Room of One's Own*. Rpt. New Delhi: Foundation, 2001.